The Bent Guide to Gay/Lesbian Canada 1995/96

CANADIAN CATALOGUING IN PUBLICATION DATA

Main entry under title:
The Bent guide to gay/lesbian Canada 1995/96

ISBN 1-55022-253-8

1. Gays — Travel — Canada — Guidebooks.
2. Lesbians — Travel — Canada — Guidebooks.
3. Gays — Services for — Canada — Guidebooks.
4. Lesbians — Services for — Canada — Guidebooks.
5. Canada — Guidebooks.
I. Title: Guide to gay/lesbian Canada 1995/96.

HQ76.3.C3B45 1995 917.104'648'08664 C95-931785-6

Design and imaging by ECW Type & Art, Oakville, Ontario.
Printed in Canada / Imprimé au Canada

Distributed by General Distribution Services,
30 Lesmill Road, Toronto, Ontario M3B 2T6,
(416) 445-3333, (800) 387-0172 (Canada), FAX (416) 445-5967.

Distributed to the trade in the United States exclusively
by InBook, 140 Commerce Street, P.O. Box 120261,
East Haven, Connecticut, U.S.A. 06512,
(203) 467-4257, FAX (203) 469-8364.
Customer service: (800) 243-0138, FAX (800) 334-3892.

Distributed in Britain by Turnaround Distribution,
27 Horsell Road, London N5 1XL,
(44) 71-609-7836, FAX (44) 71-700-1205.

Published by Bent Books and ECW PRESS,
2120 Queen Street East, Toronto, Ontario M4E 1E2.

Table of Contents

About This Guide . . . from the editors

This guide exists because a frustrated group of people realized that there has not been a gay/lesbian guide to Canada since 1988 (*Gay Canada* 88). A copy of that one can be seen at the Canadian Lesbian and Gay Archives (in Toronto, Ontario). So here is our version. We hope that next year's edition will be even bigger, as new businesses are constantly opening (although many close down just as fast). If you have any suggestions or comments, we would love your feedback. Write to us at:

Bent Books / ECW PRESS
2120 Queen Street East, Suite 200
Toronto, Ontario M4E 1E2

If you are a new business or we somehow overlooked you, let us know. We want to be as accurate as possible.

Please note that, in this guide, not all provinces will have cruising areas listed. Cruising is more discreet away from the larger urban centres. Whenever and wherever you go cruising in Canada, always be cautious and remember that sex in public places is illegal and you can be charged.

Our listings are organized alphabetically, first by province, and then by city, and then by category within city listings. We have made one exception to this rule: the four Atlantic provinces (New Brunswick, Newfoundland, Nova Scotia, and Prince Edward Island) have been combined under that heading because the less densely populated east coast offers fewer specifically gay and lesbian activities and facilities than other parts of the country.

The descriptions accompanying listings do not necessarily represent the personal opinions of the editors. For this edition we have not been able to travel all across Canada to evaluate each entry. Instead we sent out mailings and had the individual establishments write their own reviews. If there is no description with a listing, we know that the establishment exists, but the establishment has failed to respond after at least two attempts at communication on our part.

Finally we want to say that this guide was researched and written by two gay women and two gay men. This guide is for everyone. Please help us to help you, by letting us know what we could do better.

SYMBOLS

- ♿ = Wheelchair accessible
- ▼ = Establishment is gay and/or lesbian owned and/or operated

  or
- ▽ = Establishment is not gay and/or lesbian owned and/or operated, but it is gay/lesbian positive
- ⚣ = Gay male clientele
- ⚢ = Lesbian clientele
- ⚥ = Mostly straight clientele
- ♀ = Feminist clientele
- ⚧ = Mixed gay/lesbian with straight clientele

Canada — An Overview

CAPITAL: Ottawa
LARGEST PROVINCE: Ontario
OFFICIAL LANGUAGES: English & French
GOODS AND SERVICES TAX (GST): 7%
NATIONAL HOLIDAY: 1 July (Canada Day)
RELIGION: Predominantly Christian
INTERNATIONAL ACCESS CODE: 011
INTERNATIONAL COUNTRY CODE: 1

In Canada, 14 is the age of consent for sexual behaviour with a person of any age, but 18 is the age of consent for engaging in anal intercourse. Twelve- and 13-year-old persons may consent to sexual behaviour with a person between the ages of 12 and 16.

Seven of the provinces (Québec, Ontario, British Columbia, Manitoba, Saskatchewan, New Brunswick, Nova Scotia) and one of the territories (Yukon) have passed legislation in their Provincial Human Rights Codes protecting gays and lesbians from discrimination. Over the years there has been much talk of making this protection federal by adding the clause "protection against discrimination due to sexual orientation" to the Federal Human Rights Code. Justice Minister Allan Rock says that Canada isn't ready for that yet. So, we'll just have to keep working for change. As of 1992, Canada abolished its ban on allowing homosexuals to serve in the military.

Over the summer of 1994, the Ontario government voted down a bill for same-sex rights that would recognize homosexual marriages, and allow homosexual couples to receive certain benefits currently available only to straight couples. The Campaign for Equal Families, however, continues the struggle for the legal recognition of gay and lesbian marriages, and for the right for gay and lesbian couples to adopt children.

Québec is the most liberal of the provinces in its attitude towards sexuality. Contrary to popular belief, you do not have to speak French to enjoy a visit there — but many francophones will appreciate your efforts to communicate in their language.

Many retail establishments all across Canada will take American money at an exchange rate of anywhere between 10 and 20 percent. For example, $100 U.S. at a 20 percent rate of exchange would equal $120 Cdn.

The Goods and Services Tax (GST) stands all across Canada at seven percent and is paid on certain items, such as books, on top of the Provincial Sales Tax. The PST varies according to province. It will be listed in the individual provincial introductions. The GST has been in place since 1991. If you are a visitor from outside Canada, keep your receipts and your GST will be refunded to you when you leave. At duty-free shops where you see the logo "Visitor Rebate Centre," you can pick up a form to mail with your receipts when you have returned home. The minimum amount purchased must be $100 Cdn. That amount is not cumulative — it must be purchased on one trip. In Québec, you may also claim some of the PST you spend on accommodations, provided you have not stayed more than a month.

For more information on GST refunds:

Revenue Canada — Customs, Excise & Taxation
Visitor Rebate Program
Ottawa, Ontario K1A 1J5
PHONE: 1 (613) 991-3346 (if calling from outside Canada)
or, call toll-free from anywhere in Canada: 1-800-66VISIT

IMPORTANT ADDRESSES:

Canadian Accommodation Network
P.O. Box 42-A, Station M
Montréal, Québec H1V 3L6
PHONE: (514) 254-1250, FAX: (514) 252-9954

Lesbian/Gay Hospitality Exchange International
P.O. Box 612, Station C
Montréal, Québec H2L 4K5

Male Accommodation Network (MAN)
2491 Centre St.
Montréal, Québec H3K 1J9
PHONE/FAX: (514) 933-7571

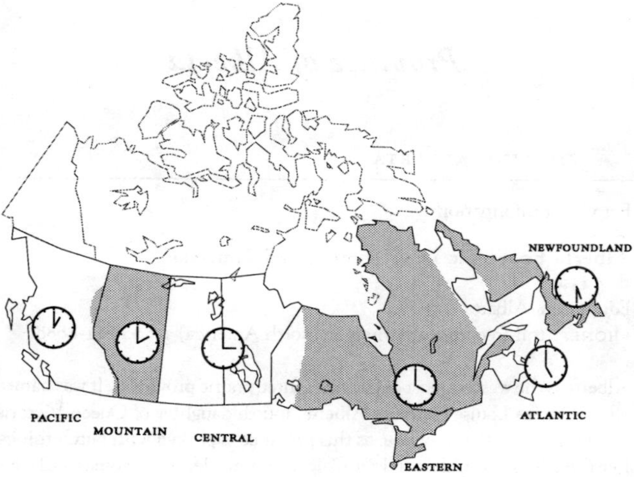

MAP OF CANADA, WITH TIME ZONES

Province of Alberta

VISITING ALBERTA

For visitor information:

Alberta Economic Development and Tourism
Box 2500
Edmonton, Alberta T5J 2Z4
PHONE: (toll-free from anywhere in North America) 1-800-661-8888

Alberta is the westernmost of Canada's three prairie provinces. It was named after Princess Louise Caroline Alberta, fourth daughter of Queen Victoria — but don't let that fool you, as this province is packed with butch things, like the Edmonton Oilers and the Calgary Stampede, and is home to kd lang, chanteuse extraordinaire.

There is no Provincial Sales Tax in Alberta, the only province without one. The legal drinking age is 18.

CALGARY: *A Brief Description*

Calgary, the city at the foot of the Rockies, boasts not only a spectacular mountain view, but a rapidly growing population of about 770,000. "Cowtown," as it is referred to by the locals, has been described as being Canada's most progressive city, as well as its most redneck.

VISITING CALGARY

For visitor information:

Calgary Convention Centre
120 – 9th Ave. S.E.
Calgary, Alberta T2G 0P3
PHONE: (403) 261-8500

For information on gay activities and services:

Apollo
P.O. Box 6481, Station D
Calgary, Alberta T2T 2E1

or at: 201 – 202, 223 – 12th Ave. S.W., T2R 0G9
PHONE: (403) 234-8973

Summers in Calgary are sunny and mild, with cool nights. Winters are long, snowy, and cold, but when those warm, dry Chinook winds slide over the Rockies, there can be a sudden rise in the temperature — surprisingly often, a –10° Celsius morning is followed by a +10° Celsius afternoon.

Your best bet for finding accommodations is an area called "The Loop," located at 13th Avenue between 6th and 7th Streets South West. Nearby, you'll find the Eighth Avenue Mall, which is the city's main walking drag, and "Electric Avenue," the nickname of 11th Avenue, the city's main strip.

Call Calgary's no-charge Accommodation Bureau at (403) 263-8510 for more information on finding a place to stay.

GETTING AROUND

Calgary International Airport is a modern facility, and there are shuttle bus and limo services to most major hotels. Also, there are the usual hotel courtesy vans. Call your hotel to find out if they offer this service.

Calgary has its own Light Rail Transit system (LRT). For route information, contact Calgary Transit at (403) 262-1000. One-way bus or C-train fare is $1.35 for adults and $0.80 for children.

Downtown parking is relatively easy with curbside meters and parking lots.

It's nearly impossible to get lost in Calgary, as the streets are laid out in a predictable grid-like manner, but watch out for those one-way streets — Calgary is a notorious "one-way" town.

Calgary is exceedingly cycle-friendly. Its city streets are safe and quiet. Parks have extensive paths, including Prince's Island, 10 minutes from the city centre. A cycling route map is available from City of Calgary Parks and Recreation, at (403) 268-5211.

GAY PLACES OF INTEREST

For the gay or lesbian visitor to Calgary, there is no shortage of things to see and do.

There are many gay bars, gay-friendly restaurants, saunas, bookstores, and shops to visit.

Calgary's Lesbian and Gay Pride Day is usually celebrated on the last Sunday in June, but call the local gayline to be sure.

For more information, see the complete listing for Calgary in this guide.

ENTERTAINMENT

For those of you into leather chaps and harnesses, the world-famous Calgary Stampede is for you. It's one of the largest rodeos in the world, with enough cowpokes to keep you two-stepping till the cows come home. It is held in July, and lasts for 10 days.

For the cultural connoisseur, there is the Calgary Centre for Performing Arts, which is home to the Calgary Philharmonic Orchestra and the city's two main professional theatre companies, Alberta Theatre Projects and Theatre Calgary.

Visit the Olympic Saddledome, site of the 1988 Winter Games.

For those who like to watch things grow, visit Devonian Gardens, a beautiful indoor garden in the heart of downtown Calgary. It is also connected to some *fabulous* shopping.

If you go for furry animals, take in the Calgary Zoo. It is the second-largest zoo in Canada, includes a prehistoric park, and it is fierce.

CRUISING AREAS

Some of Calgary's popular cruising areas include the east end of Prince's Island at 4th Street, but exercise caution. The Loop, at 13th Avenue between 6th and 7th Streets South West, is also a prime area for cruising.

As well, Stanley Park, just off Elbow Drive, near 4th Avenue South West, offers some good cruising action.

At the University of Calgary, the men's washrooms are a popular spot for cruising, but remember, washroom sex is illegal in Canada, so do it at your own risk.

Calgary, Alberta (403)

ACCOMMODATION/BED & BREAKFAST

Delta Bow Valley
209 – 4th Ave. S.E., T2G 0C6
PHONE:: 266-1980, FAX: 266-0007
The Delta Bow Valley is a four-diamond deluxe facility located in the downtown business core of Calgary. Enjoy your visit in one of the 398 spacious guest rooms or utilize the fitness and meeting rooms, restaurants, or lounge. Continental food served.
RATES: Starting at $99
PAYMENT: cash, traveller's cheques, American Express, MasterCard, VISA
♿ ▽ ⚥

Renaud House
605 – 10th Ave. N.E., T2E 0X9
PHONE: 277-0672
A very comfortable, clean, and bright one-bedroom apartment, fully equipped with a private entrance. Close to downtown. Owned by a friendly lesbian couple always aware of "what's on" in town — ask for Barb or Pat, or leave a message.
▼ ⚣ ⚢

Westways Guesthouse
216 – 25th Ave. S.W., T2S 0L1
PHONE/FAX: 229-1758
Edwardian heritage home with friendly charm. Ten-minute walk to nearest gay bars. Buses and trains close by. Parking and hot tub available. Rooms with private bathroom available.
RATES: $50 to $65 single, $60 to $80 double
PAYMENT: cash, American Express, VISA
▼ ⚤

Arena
310 – 17th Ave. S.W., T2S 0A8
PHONE: 228-5730
▼ ⚣

Boystown
213 – 10th Ave. S.W., T2R 0A4
PHONE: 265-2028
Video cruise bar.
HOURS: Daily from 9:00 p.m.
PAYMENT: cash, American Express, MasterCard, VISA
▼ ⚣

BBX Complex
1207 – 1st St. S.W., T2R 0V3
PHONE: 237-7187
⚣ ⚢

Detour
318 – 17th Ave. S.W., T2S 0A8
PHONE: 244-8537
HOURS: Closed Monday and Tuesday
PAYMENT: cash, traveller's cheques, American Express, MasterCard, VISA
▼ ⚣ ⚢

Rekroom
213-A – 10th Ave. S.W., T2R 0A4
PHONE: 265-4749
Video cruise bar.
HOURS: Daily from 4:00 p.m.
PAYMENT: cash, American Express, MasterCard, VISA
▼ ⚣

Trax Private Club
1130 – 10th Ave. S.W., T2R 0B6
PHONE: 245-8477

BATHS/SAUNAS

Goliath's Saunatel
308 – 17th Ave. S.W., T2S 0A8
PHONE: 229-0911

BOOKSHOPS/LIBRARIES

After Dark
(See entry under RETAIL heading.)

Self-Connection Books
4004 – 19th St. N.W., T2L 2B6
PHONE: 284-1486

Tad's Bookstore
1217-A – 9th Ave. S.E., T2G 0S9
PHONE: 237-8237

Woman's Place Bookstore
1412 Center St. S., T2G 2E4
PHONE: 263-5256, FAX: 263-5257
Large selection of lesbian and gay books. Only women's bookstore in Alberta. Special orders are welcome by phone or fax.
HOURS: Monday to Sunday 10:00 a.m. – 6:00 p.m.
PAYMENT: cash, personal or traveller's cheques, American Express, MasterCard, VISA
♿ ▼ ♀ ⚧

CHURCHES/RELIGIOUS ORGANIZATIONS

Unitarian Universalist Church
1703 – 1st St. N.W., T2M 4P4
PHONE: 276-2436
▽

GALLERIES

New Zones Gallery
803 – 24th Ave. S.E., T2G 1P5
PHONE: 266-1972, FAX: 258-0719

HEALTH CLUBS

Goliath's
308 – 17th Ave. S.W., T2S 0A8
PHONE: 229-0911

PUBLICATIONS

Outword!
Pride Publishing, Inc.
1412 Centre St. S., T2G 2E4
PHONE: 237-5227, FAX: 237-5253
E-mail: PRIDE.PUBLISHING@CIA.COM
Alberta's monthly news and lifestyle magazine for the gay, lesbian, and bisexual community. Includes features and comprehensive listings. Subscriptions are available.
HOURS: Monday to Friday 10:00 a.m. – 3:00 p.m.
PAYMENT: cash, money orders, personal and traveller's cheques
▼ ⚣ ⚢

Unity Pages
P.O. Box 1413, Station M, T2P 2L6
PHONE: 282-6540
Western Canada's only gay and lesbian business directory, distributed locally, nationally, and internationally.
PAYMENT: cheques
▼ ⚣ ⚢

RESTAURANTS/CAFÉS

Entre Nous Restaurant
2206 – 4th St. S.W., T2S 1W9
PHONE: 228-5525, FAX: 245-2402
Atmosphere, ambiance, and marvellous food are what make Entre Nous a popular spot in Calgary. Reservations are requested.
French continental cuisine.
HOURS: Monday to Friday lunch 11:30 a.m. – 1:30 p.m.
Monday to Saturday dinner 6:00 p.m. – close
PAYMENT: cash, traveller's cheques, American Express, MasterCard, VISA
♿ ▽ ⚥

Grabbajabba
1610 – 10th St. S.W., T2R 1G1
PHONE: 244-7750
A friendly coffeehouse. Unique eye-opening design. Drop by for your early morning pick-me-up, lunch, or after dinner for coffee and dessert.
HOURS: Monday to Thursday 7:00 a.m. – 11:00 p.m.
Friday 7:00 a.m. – midnight
Saturday 8:00 a.m. – midnight
Sunday 9:00 a.m. – 11:00 p.m.
(until midnight every night during the summer)
PAYMENT: cash, personal and traveller's cheques
♿ ▽ ⚥

The Little Place Restaurant
1130-A Kensington Rd. N.W., T2N 3P3
PHONE: 283-4121
A fresh-food restaurant specializing in custom-order sandwiches on home-baked bread. Great all-day Sunday brunch.
HOURS: Monday to Friday 8:00 a.m. – 5:00 p.m.
Saturday 9:00 a.m. – 5:00 p.m.
Sunday 9:00 a.m. – 4:00 p.m.
PAYMENT: cash, personal and traveller's cheques
▽ ⚥

Lyon's Empire Inc.
940A – 11th Ave. S.W., T2R 0E7
PHONE: 228-0818

Max Beanies Coffee Bar
1410 – 4th St. S.W., T2R 0Y1
PHONE: 237-6185

Victoria's Restaurant
306 – 17th Ave. S.W., T2S 0A8
PHONE: 244-9991
Mixed clientele. Established in 1986. Home cooking.
HOURS: Sunday to Thursday 11:00 a.m. – midnight
Friday and Saturday 11:00 a.m. – 2:00 a.m.
PAYMENT: cash, traveller's cheques, American Express, MasterCard, Visa
♿ ▼ ⚥

RETAIL

After Dark *or* **After Dark Adult Warehouse**
1314 – 1st St. S.W., T2R 0V7 7248 Ogden Rd. S.E., T2C 1B6
PHONE: 264-SEXY (7399), FAX: 269-4251
Calgary's oldest complete adult store — now in its 15th year. 1st Street location has peep shows and private viewing rooms.
HOURS: 1st Street: Monday to Friday 10:00 a.m. – midnight
Ogden Road: Monday to Saturday noon – midnight
PAYMENT: cash, traveller's cheques, American Express, MasterCard, VISA
♿ ▼ ⚥

B&B Leatherworks / Lingerie by Barbie
6802 Ogden Rd. S.E., T2C 1B4
PHONE: 236-7072, FAX: 236-1304
B&B stocks: custom clothing, fetish costumes, PVC, corsets, maid outfits, rubberwear, leather, stilettos, feminization. Only limited by your imagination. Catalogues are available. Mail orders accepted.
HOURS: Tuesday to Friday 9:30 a.m. – 6:00 p.m.
Saturday 1:00 p.m. – 6:00 p.m.
PAYMENT: cash, personal and traveller's cheques, VISA
▽ ⚥

Erogenous Zone
3812 Macleod Tr. S.E., T2G 2R2
PHONE: 287-3100

Galleria Arts & Crafts
1141 Kensington Rd. N.W., T2N 3P4
PHONE: 270-3612

Stairway Leathers
210 – 4th Ave. N.E., T2E 0J1
PHONE: 276-2471

With the Times
2212A – 4th St. S.W., T2S 1W9
PHONE: 244-8020, FAX: 244-8019
Retailer of more than two thousand magazines, including gay and lesbian titles. Also sells newspapers, pocketbooks, and greeting cards.
♿ ▼ ⚥

SERVICES

AIDS Calgary Awareness Association

300, 1021 – 10th Ave. S.W., T2R 0B7

PHONE: 228-0155, FAX: 229-2077

ACAA is a volunteer-based, nonprofit health organization. The agency's mandate is to increase awareness of HIV infection and AIDS.

♿ ▽ ⚦

C.L.U.B. Calgary

201, 223 – 12th Ave. S.W., T2R 0G9

PHONE: 234-8973

An organization that promotes community and fund-raising. Offers volunteers for other community groups when needed.

▽ ⚦

Gay Lines Calgary

201, 223 – 12th Ave. S.W., T2R 0G9

PHONE: 234-8973, FAX: 261-9776

Gay Lines offers information to the gay/lesbian/bisexual communities and peer-counselling and referral services for gay and bisexual men. Information on local clubs, gay/lesbian-positive businesses, and community events, as well as information on other cities and countries. Gay Lines also operates a drop-in and library. Call ahead for wheelchair accessibility.

HOURS: Daily 7:00 p.m. – 10:00 p.m.

♿ ▼ ⚣

Lesbian Information Line

210, 223 – 12th Ave. S.W., T2R 0G9

PHONE: 265-9458

Operated by the Womyn's Collective Social & Recreational Society.

HOURS: Monday and Wednesday 7:30 p.m. – 9:30 p.m.

PFLAG

20 Hendon Dr. N.W., T2K 1Y5

PHONE: Tom Rash 282-6592

TRAVEL/TOURS

Fletcher Scott

PHONE: 332-1180

[*Editor's note*: Will be moving. Call number for new number and address.]

Stonewall Connection
302 Sharon Ave. S.W., T3C 2G7
PHONE: 244-7773, FAX: 244-7748

The Travel Group
2306 – 14A St. S.W., T2T 3X1
PHONE: 541-1951, FAX: 541-1952
Parent company of full-service travel agency.
HOURS: Monday to Saturday 8:00 a.m. – 6:00 p.m.
PAYMENT: cash, personal and traveller's cheques, American Express, MasterCard, VISA
♿ ▼ ⚣ ⚢

Triangle Tours
c/o 1000, 717 – 7th Ave. S.W., T2P 0Z3
PHONE: 234-0463, FAX: 269-5370
[*Editor's note*: At time of publication, this business was planning to open soon, but had not yet.]

Uniglobe Swift Travel
112, 908 – 17th Ave. S.W., T2T 0A3
PHONE: 244-7887, FAX: 229-2611
An established travel agency since 1988. Serving the gay and lesbian community across Canada. Please call for tour information.
HOURS: Monday to Friday 8:30 a.m. – 5:00 p.m.
From 15 September – 30 April also open Saturday 10:00 a.m. – 3:30 p.m.
PAYMENT: cash, personal and traveller's cheques, American Express, En Route, MasterCard
▽ ⚥

OTHER

Almost Magic
802 Edmonton Trail N.E., T2E 3J6
PHONE: 230-5425
Friendly, bright salon, five large tanning rooms, drop-in's welcome. Good parking. Central.
♿ ▼ ⚥

CJSW 90.9 FM
"Speak Sebastian"
HOURS: Wednesday 9:00 p.m. – 10:00 p.m.

EDMONTON: *A Brief Description*

Called the "Gateway to the North," and located in the heart of Alberta, Edmonton is the province's capital city. With a population of about 850,000, Edmonton is also Alberta's most densely populated city. It's also the home of the Edmonton Oilers.

VISITING EDMONTON

For visitor information:

Edmonton Convention and Tourism
104, 9797 Jasper Ave.
Edmonton, Alberta T5J 1N9
PHONE: (403) 426-4715

Contact the Edmonton gayline at (403) 488-3234, or visit the Gay/Lesbian Community Centre at 104, 11745 Jasper Avenue in Edmonton.

Summer is sunny, windy, and temperatures fluctuate from hot to cool. Winter in Edmonton is cold and snowy, so dig out your sexiest winter-wear, and go out and generate some heat.

GETTING AROUND

Edmonton International Airport offers taxi and limo services to the city's downtown core. Check with your hotel to see if they offer courtesy vans.

Edmonton has its own metro bus system and LRT. The cost is $1.50 for adults and $0.70 for children. For route information, call Edmonton Transportation at (403) 421-4636.

Like Calgary, Edmonton is extremely cycle-friendly, with dozens of paths to explore. Call the Edmonton Information Centre at (403) 426-4715 for route details.

GAY PLACES OF INTEREST

Gay Pride Day festivities are usually carried out on the last Sunday in June. Contact the gayline for more information.

Visit the gay and lesbian bars and bookstores, and drop by Executive-Express, a video store catering specifically to gay males.

ENTERTAINMENT

Cultural facilities in Edmonton include the Edmonton Symphony Society, the Edmonton Opera Association, and the Citadel Theatre.

Visitors who like their theatre a little more on the edge can go to the Fringe Theatre Event, a nine-day showcase for local, regional, and international performing artists. It attracts up to 175,000 people per year, ranking it the third-largest festival of its kind in the world.

Don't forget the West Edmonton Mall, the world's largest mall, with a zoo, a wave park, and over 800 stores. You'll shop till you drop and beg for mercy in this suburban queer's paradise.

CRUISING AREAS

Edmonton's cruising areas include Victoria Park, near the golf course, at your own risk, and the hill across from the Macdonald Hotel. River Road, near the Victoria Golf Course, offers some exciting cruising, as well as Alberta College Parking Lot, located on Macdonald Drive (at your own risk).

Edmonton, Alberta (403)

ACCOMMODATION/BED & BREAKFAST

Northern Lights B&B
Box 515, T5J 2K1
PHONE: 483-1572
Quiet antique guest rooms in a spacious and comfortable home. Heated pool, close to West Edmonton Mall, 15 minutes from downtown. Please call Alfredo for reservations.
RATES: $45 single, $55 double
PAYMENT: cash
▼ ⚣ ⚢

BARS

Boots and Saddles
10242 – 106 St., T5J 1H7
PHONE: 423-5014
⚣

Option Room
10148 – 105 St., T5J 1C9
PHONE: 423-4666
HOURS: Wednesday to Saturday 8:00 p.m. – 4:00 a.m.
⚥

The Roost
10345 – 104 St., T5J 1B9
PHONE: 426-3150, FAX: 487-6138
This is a disco bar with two levels. On weekends the second floor is open with disco upstairs and western downstairs. There is a patio for summer use. There is also a deli. Good service available. The Roost supports other gay organizations in Edmonton and area.
HOURS: Monday to Sunday 8:00 p.m. – 3:00 a.m.
PAYMENT: cash, traveller's cheques, INTERAC, MasterCard, VISA
♿ ▼ ⚥

BOOKSHOPS/LIBRARIES

Audrey's Books Ltd.
10702 Jasper Ave., T5J 3J5
PHONE: 423-3487, FAX: 425-8446
A full-service general bookstore with a strong selection of books dealing with gay and lesbian issues as well as gay and lesbian fiction. Mail orders are accepted.
♿ ▽ ⚥

Greenwood's Bookshoppe
10355 Whyte Ave., T6E 1Z9
PHONE: 439-2005, FAX: 433-5774
Toll-Free (Canada-wide): 1-800-661-2078
Large independent bookstore in Edmonton offering a good selection of gay/lesbian fiction and non-fiction in the heart of Old Strathcona. Mail orders accepted.

HOURS: Monday to Friday 9:30 a.m. – 9:00 p.m.
Saturday 9:30 a.m. – 5:30 p.m.
Sunday noon – 4:00 p.m.
PAYMENT: cash, personal and traveller's cheques, Debit Card, American Express, MasterCard, VISA
♿ ▽ ⚥

Orlando Books Ltd.

10640 Whyte Ave., T6E 2A7
PHONE: 432-7633, FAX: 439-9878
This is a general bookstore with depth in certain areas: literary fiction, reference, poetry, science, music, women's issues, gay and lesbian titles, philosophy, left-wing politics, peace issues, First Nations, vegetarian cookbooks, and good children's books. Special orders are welcome. Friday night events. Each month the store sponsors a different charity.
HOURS: Monday to Wednesday 10:00 a.m. – 6:00 p.m.
Thursday and Friday 10:00 a.m. – 9:00 p.m.
Saturday 10:00 a.m. – 6:00 p.m.
PAYMENT: cash, Debit Card, American Express, MasterCard, VISA
▽ ⚢⚣

Varscona Books

10309 Whyte Ave.
PHONE: 439-4195

Woman-to-Womon Books

106, 12404 – 114 Ave., T5M 3M5
PHONE: 454-8031

CHURCHES/RELIGIOUS ORGANIZATIONS

Integrity

Box 35010, Oliver Post Office, T5K 2R8
PHONE: 425-9017

Lutherans Concerned

P.O. Box 11095, T5J 3K4
PHONE: 426-2533 (Tom)
A society for gay/lesbian Christians and "friends of." Working to foster a climate of justice, understanding, and reconciliation among all women and men. Meets monthly.
⚣ ⚢

Metropolitan Community Church of Edmonton
PHONE: 429-2321
For all people. Worships at 10086 Macdonald Drive on Sundays at 7:15 p.m.
⚣ ⚢

GALLERIES

Boystown Café Gallery
10116 – 124 St., T5N 1P6
PHONE: 488-6636

MUSEUMS/ARCHIVES

Edmonton Gay & Lesbian Archives
c/o GLCCE
104, 11745 Jasper Ave., *or* Mailing address: P.O. Box 1852, T5K 2P2
PHONE: 488-3234

PUBLICATIONS

Greater Edmonton Pride Pages
P.O. Box 1852, T5K 2P2
PHONE: 488-3234
▼ ⚣ ⚢

Times .10 Magazine
Box 932, T5J 2L8
PHONE: 431-1333

RESTAURANTS/CAFÉS

Common Ground
10203 – 116 St. N.W., T5K 1W3
PHONE: 482-3063

Executive-Express

201, 10120 – 118th St., T5K 1Y4

PHONE: 482-7480

The only completely gay video store in western Canada: video rentals, sales, and mail order, clothing, leathers, and other essentials for the gay life-style.

HOURS: Daily (except Tuesday) 1:00 p.m. – 9:00 p.m.

PAYMENT: cash, VISA

▼ ⚣

Express Yourself

Mailing address: 412, 10145 – 121 St., T5N 1K5

PHONE/FAX: 488-7920

Edmonton's only one-stop source for t-shirts, jewellery, body jewellery, notebooks, cards, and much more for the lesbigay community. A mobile store — call us for our next location.

PAYMENT: cash, cheques

▼ ⚣ ⚢

Fable Video

706 – 9th St. S.W., T2P 2B4

PHONE: 292-0299

For Play Adult Boutique

10524 – 124 St., T5N 1R9

PHONE: 482-4066, FAX: 482-4337

Stockists of quality leather and custom latex fashion and accessories. A wide selection of B&D/S&M equipment, manuals, import magazines, corsetry, shoes, boots, and toys. Not to be missed while in Edmonton. Mail orders are accepted.

HOURS: Monday to Friday noon – 8:00 p.m.

PAYMENT: cash, INTERAC, MasterCard, VISA

♿ ▽ ⚥

The Front Page

10846 Jasper Ave., T5J 2B2

PHONE: 426-1206

The Front Page is downtown Edmonton's newest and largest magazine and newspaper retail store, catering to the community at large with a good collection of gay and lesbian, feminist, and alternative titles.

HOURS: Monday to Wednesday, Friday 8:30 a.m. – 7:00 p.m.
Thursday 8:30 a.m. – 8:00 p.m.
Saturday 9:30 a.m. – 7:00 p.m.
PAYMENT: cash, personal and traveller's cheques, MasterCard, VISA
♿ ▼ ⚦

Lyon's Empire Inc.
10121 – 124 St., T5N 1P5
PHONE: 488-6915

Movies & More
8211 – 102 St. S.W., T6E 4A5
PHONE: 433-6231

SERVICES

AIDS Network of Edmonton Society (a social service agency)
201, 11456 Jasper Ave., T5K 0M1
PHONE: 488-5742, FAX: 488-3735
Offers support services to people affected by HIV infection/AIDS, an info line, counselling, referrals, support groups, preventive education programs, a resource centre, a speaker's bureau, a gay men's outreach project, advocacy, and public awareness programs.
♿ ▽ ⚦

Gay and Lesbian Community Centre of Edmonton (GLCCE)
104, 11745 Jasper Ave.
Mailing address:
Gay and Lesbian Community Centre of Edmonton
P.O. Box 1852, Edmonton, Alberta T5K 2P2
PHONE: 488-3234
HOURS: Monday to Friday 7:00 p.m. – 10:00 p.m.
Wednesday 1:00 p.m. – 4:00 p.m.
OTHER SERVICES OFFERED:
Gay events line: 988-4018
Youth info line: 488-1574
The Gay and Lesbian Community Centre of Edmonton is a drop-in centre, offering peer counselling, a six-hundred-book library, information boards, and publications by groups in the Edmonton area. The GLCCE publishes a monthly newsletter.
▼ ⚣ ⚢

Gayline
PHONE: 486-9661

PFLAG
PHONE: 462-5958 (Lynne)
Meets the third Tuesday of every month.

Womonspace/Lesbian Lifeline
PHONE: 425-0511
Organizes dances and events. Women's membership is $15 Cdn. annually.
▼ ♀ ⚢

TRAVEL/TOURS

Encore Holidays
260, 8170 – 50 St. N.W., T6B 1E6
PHONE: 468-9439

West End Travel
15803 – 87 Ave. N.W., T5R 4G7
PHONE: 483-9124

OTHER

CJSR (Gaywire)
FM 88.5
PHONE: 492-5244
HOURS: Thursday nights at 6:00 p.m.

Grand Prairie, Alberta (403)

SERVICES

Peace Gay/Lesbian Association
PHONE: 539-3325

Lethbridge, Alberta (403)

SERVICES

Gay/Lesbian Association of Lethbridge
Box 2081, T1J 4K6
PHONE: 329-4666

Gay/Lesbian Peer Support Line
PHONE: 329-4666, FAX: 328-8564
Provides support and referrals for the Lethbridge and area gay, lesbian, and bisexual community. Staffed Wednesday, 7:00 p.m. to 10:00 p.m., with an answering machine at other times. Messages are answered immediately.

Lighthouse Social Group
PHONE: 329-8273

Red Deer, Alberta (403)

BARS

The Other Place (T.O.P.)
Bay 3&4, 5579 – 47th St., T4N 1S1
PHONE: 342-6440
Full menu available, pool tables, dance floor, and a D.J. on weekends.
HOURS: Daily 4:00 p.m. – 3:00 a.m.
PAYMENT: cash
♿ ▼ ⚣ ⚢

BOOKSHOPS/LIBRARIES

Rainbow Books
P.O. Box 24020, Plaza Centre P.O., T4N 6X6
PHONE: 341-6616

SERVICES

GALACA: Gay/Lesbian Association of Central Alberta
PHONE: 340-2198

Atlantic Provinces — New Brunswick, Newfoundland, Nova Scotia, and Prince Edward Island

The gay scene in the Atlantic provinces is very discreet, but starting to become more active. *Gaezette*, the gay and lesbian newspaper serving the Atlantic provinces, is based in Halifax, Nova Scotia. There are a few gay bars in other areas, but most of the action is located in the Halifax, Nova Scotia, area. Pride Week celebrations, although not held in Newfoundland, are usually in the last week of June, with most of the festivities happening in Halifax. There is a parade through the streets of Halifax on Gay and Lesbian Pride Day, with dances and parties scheduled.

There is really no "gay scene" in Prince Edward Island, although there are a couple of bars in Charlottetown where local gays and lesbians tend to hang out.

Newfoundland, like Prince Edward Island, also lacks a defined gay and lesbian scene.

New Brunswick has a couple of gay and lesbian bars to visit.

VISITING *New Brunswick*

For visitor information:

New Brunswick Tourism
P.O. Box 12345
Fredericton, New Brunswick E3B 5C3
PHONE: 1-800-561-0123

New Brunswick's summer months are June, July, and August, and the summers are usually warm in the days and cool at night. September and October are cooler, and medium-weight clothing is recommended. Winters are cold, wet, and snowy.

The Provincial Sales Tax in New Brunswick is 11 percent. The legal drinking age is 19.

GETTING AROUND NEW BRUNSWICK

Fredericton Airport is located five miles outside of Fredericton.

The SMT is New Brunswick's province-wide transit system, and users are charged according to the distance travelled on the system.

All out-of-province visitors to Fredericton can get a free Tourist Parking Pass, available year-round from the Visitor Information Centre, at City Hall on Queen Street in Fredericton, New Brunswick. The passes permit free parking at all municipal parking meters and car parks in Fredericton. People driving rental cars from New Brunswick can get a pass by showing proof of out-of-province residency, and by presenting a copy of the rental agreement.

GAY PLACES OF INTEREST

For lesbian and gay visitors to New Brunswick, there are only two lesbian and gay bars: Kurt's Dance Warehouse, in Fredericton, and Dans l'Fond, in Moncton, which caters to both lesbians and gay men.

ENTERTAINMENT

There's a lot to see and do year-round in New Brunswick.

When visiting Fredericton, culture buffs will enjoy The Playhouse, home of the province's only professional theatre company, The Theatre New Brunswick.

During the summer months, Officer's Square, on Queen Street, is one of Fredericton's most scenic areas. Here you can see summer band concerts and outdoor theatre performances at no charge.

Campers will enjoy the thick forests of Fredericton's Mactaquac park, overlooking Mactaquac Dam.

At Fredericton's City Hall, you can see the spot where Oscar Wilde lectured, and the fountain with the ornamental cherub on top of it, nicknamed "Freddie, the little nude dude."

There are things to do outside of Fredericton, as well.

In June, go to Oromocto for the New Brunswick Highland Games, and find out just what is under those kilts.

July is the time of the Lobster Festival in Shediac (for all you fish lovers), and the International Festival of Baroque Music in Lamèque.

For you travellers who like to have something sweet in your mouth, in August there's the International Festival and Chocolate Fest in St. Stephen.

In Saint John, visit the New Brunswick Museum, Canada's oldest museum and host of many fine cultural, historical, and scientific exhibits.

CRUISING AREAS

The cruising areas in Fredericton include Regent Mall and Riverside Park, which is located between Lord Beaverbrook Hotel and the Railway Bridge.

Aulac, New Brunswick (506)

ACCOMMODATION/BED & BREAKFAST

Georgian House
RR#3, Sackville, E0A 3C0
PHONE: 536-1481
A restored 1840 home appointed with mostly Georgian and Victorian antiques. It is nestled in a quiet country environment five minutes off the junction of Aulac Interchange.
RATES: $45 to $50
PAYMENT: cash, traveller's cheques
▼ ♀

Bathurst, New Brunswick (506)

SERVICES

Gai.es Nor Gays Inc.
P.O. Box 983, E2A 4H8
PHONE: 783-7440
This is an incorporated association serving gays and lesbians of northern New Brunswick. The association's goal is to break the isolation common in rural areas. Dances and other activities are organized for that purpose. A phone line with a phone box is also available. Interactive phone-line night is on Friday from 8:00 p.m. to 10:00 p.m. A newsletter is published 10 times a year.

Fredericton, New Brunswick (506)

BARS

Kurt's Dance Warehouse
353 Queen St., E3B 1B1
PHONE: 453-0740, FAX: 458-8764
Bar and dance club. Down the alley.
HOURS: Thursday 8:00 p.m. – 1:00 a.m.
Friday and Saturday 8:00 p.m. – 2:00 a.m.
PAYMENT: cash, MasterCard, VISA
♿ ▼ ⚣ ⚢

BOOKSHOPS/LIBRARIES

Westminster Books
445 King St., E3B 1E5
PHONE: 454-1442, FAX: 452-9330

SERVICES

FLAG
P.O. Box 1556, Station A, E3B 5G2
PHONE: 457-2156
Meets the second Wednesday of each month on the University of New Brunswick campus. Phone line is from 7:00 p.m. to 9:00 p.m. on Mondays and Thursdays. Counselling and support.

Gayline
PHONE: 457-2156
HOURS: Monday and Thursday 6:00 p.m. – 9:00 p.m.
Contact the Gayline for MCC and the local FLAG group.

Moncton, New Brunswick (506)

BARS

Dans L'Fond
234 St. George St., E1C 1V9
⚣ ⚢

SERVICES

Gays and Lesbians of Moncton Line
P.O. Box 1072, Riverview, E1B 1V0
PHONE: 855-8064
HOURS: Monday and Thursday 7:00 p.m. – 9:00 p.m.

Saint John, New Brunswick (506)

ACCOMMODATION/BED & BREAKFAST

Mahogany Manor
220 Germain St., E2L 2G4
PHONE: 636-8000
Walking distance to downtown Saint John. Spacious living areas in a turn-of-the-century home. Queen- or king-sized beds, private baths, and heirloom furniture pieces. Full breakfast included.
RATES: $55 to $65
PAYMENT: cash, traveller's cheques, MasterCard
▼ ⚥

VISITING *Newfoundland*

For visitor information:

Department of Tourism and Culture Newfoundland
P.O. Box 8730
St. John's, Newfoundland A1B 4K2
PHONE: (709) 729-2830

The climate of the island varies depending on where you're staying. The west coast is almost always sunny, while the southeast is usually damp and foggy. This is due to the warm, moist winds of the Gulf Stream mixing with the cold air over the Labrador Current from the Arctic Ocean.

In St. John's, winters are very cold, and summers are on the cool side. Bring a sexy sweater to warm up in.

The most recommended time of the year to visit Newfoundland is during the summer months, when the green, natural beauty of the many capes, bays, and valleys makes a truly breathtaking sight.

Newfoundland's Provincial Sales Tax is 12 percent, the highest in Canada, so budget carefully. The legal drinking age is 19.

GETTING AROUND NEWFOUNDLAND

Newfoundland is served by airports located at St. John's, Stephenville, Deer Lake, Labrador City, and Gander. Only taxis are available to take you to the city centres, as there is no bus service.

There is a ferry that operates between North Sydney, Nova Scotia, and Channel-Port aux Basques on the southwest coast, where it connects with the highway to St. John's.

To truly appreciate the natural beauty and sensual sights of the province, we recommend you tour Newfoundland by car.

GAY PLACES OF INTEREST

There are a few bars for gays and lesbians located in St. John's, including Zone 216 and the Back Alley Pub.

ENTERTAINMENT

St. John's is home to many museums and art galleries located along Water and Duckworth Streets.

The LSPU Hall in St. John's is a venue for alternative theatre, and is the original home of CODCO, and is very gay-positive.

At the entrance to St. John's harbour is Signal Hill, a major tourist attraction.

For winter visitors, good skiing can be had at Marble Mountain, near Corner Brook.

CRUISING AREAS

Cruising is done around the gay bars of the area, the Back Alley Pub, and Zone 216.

St. John's, Newfoundland (709)

BARS

Back Alley Pub
164B Water St., A1C 1A9
PHONE: 726-6782
⚥

Schroder's Piano Bar
10 Bates Hill, A1C 4B4
PHONE: 753-0807
[*Editor's note*: Jazz bar that some gay couples enjoy.]
⚥ ⚣ ⚢

Zone 216
216 Water St., A1C 1A9
PHONE: 754-2492
[*Editor's note*: The main bar for gays and lesbians.]
⚣ ⚢ ⚥

BOOKSHOPS/LIBRARIES

Wordplay
221 Duckworth St., A1C 1G7
PHONE: 726-9193
⚥

RESTAURANTS/CAFÉS

Zapata's
10 Bates Hill, A1C 4B4
PHONE: 753-6215
[*Editor's note*: Below Schroder's Piano Bar. Mexican food.]
⚥

SERVICES

Newfoundland & Labrador AIDS Committee Inc.
P.O. Box 626, Station C, A1C 5K8
PHONE: 579-8656
Contact gay outreach group through this number for more information on local bars: Back Alley Pub, Schroder's Piano Bar, and Zone 216.

TRAVEL/TOURS

Planet Travel
P.O. Box 552
Gander, Newfoundland A1V 2E1
PHONE: 256-9385, FAX: 256-9375
Toll-Free: 1-800-667-2642
A full-service travel and tours agency, proudly serving Atlantic Canada's gay and lesbian community.
▼ ⚣ ⚢

VISITING *Nova Scotia*

For visitor information:

Tourism Halifax Information Centre
City Hall
Duke St. at Barrington (opposite Scotia Square)
PHONE: (902) 421-8736

Summers in Halifax are sunny and cool, perfect for vacationing, while winters are wet, cold, damp, and snowy. The Provincial Sales Tax for Nova Scotia is 11 percent. The legal drinking age is 19.

GETTING AROUND NOVA SCOTIA

Halifax airport serves the province, and Nova Scotia has a metro bus system, with a single adult fare costing about $1.50.

Taxi services are also widely available.

GAY PLACES OF INTEREST

Halifax seems to be the hub of the gay and lesbian community in the Atlantic provinces. There are many gay and lesbian bars, a gay newspaper, bookstores, and a gay and lesbian information line.

Gay Pride Week is usually celebrated during the last week in June, with dances, films, and people and things to see.

Central Halifax is the location of the city's gay community, which is concentrated around the gay bars.

ENTERTAINMENT

Halifax is the location of the Art Gallery of Nova Scotia, and the Neptune Theatre, which offers about half-a-dozen different productions between September and May.

Jazz East, the province's jazz festival, is held in mid-July.

Don't miss the exciting Atlantic Winter Fair, held in early October.

CRUISING AREAS

The most cruising is done around the centre of the gay community in downtown Halifax, near the gay bars. Also check out Citadel Hill, Crystal Crescent Beach, and the Public Gardens.

Bear River, Nova Scotia (902)

ACCOMMODATION/BED & BREAKFAST

Lovett Lodge Inn
P.O. Box 119, Main St., BOS 1BO
PHONE: 467-3917
Toll-Free: 1-800-565-0000 (within Canada)
1-800-341-6096 (from the U.S.A.)
A Victorian doctor's residence situated in an Alpine setting on Tidal River. Antiques, library, art, and music. Near the Digby ferry, National Park, and historic Annapolis Royal. Hwy 101, exit 24 or 25 (Evangeline Trail). Full breakfast and evening tea is included. Open 15 May to 31 October.
RATES: $35 single, $40 double, $44 twin, $8 extra per extra person, $6 extra for a private bath
▽ ⚧

Halifax, Nova Scotia (902)

ACCOMMODATION/BED & BREAKFAST

Bob's B&B
2715 Windsor St., B3K 5E1
PHONE: 454-4374

Centretown Bed & Breakfast
2016 Oxford St., B3L 2T2
PHONE: 422-2380

A 1920s-style bungalow with a front veranda, located in the heart of the city with major bus routes converging on the street corners of Oxford and Quinpool. The immediate neighbourhood has English, French, Greek, Indian, Chinese, and Spanish residents. Rumours bar is 10 blocks away and the local cruising area is seven blocks away.

RATES: $50 to $65 in season, $40 to $50 off season

PAYMENT: cash, traveller's cheques, MasterCard, VISA

▼ ⚤

Fresh Start B&B

2720 Gottingen St., B3K 3C7

PHONE: 453-6616, FAX: 453-6617

Victorian house. Informal atmosphere, great breakfast at your convenience, and flexible check-in and check-out.

RATES: $40 to $70

PAYMENT: cash, personal and traveller's cheques, American Express, MasterCard, VISA

▽ ⚤

BARS

Rumours Club

2112 Gottingen St., B3K 3B3

PHONE: 423-6814

Rumours is a large dance club and bar for gays and lesbians and their friends. It is owned and operated by the Gay and Lesbian Association of Nova Scotia.

▼ ⚣ ⚢

Seahorse Tavern

1665 Argyle St., B3J 3K4

The Studio

1537 Barrington St., B3J 1Z4

PHONE: 423-6866

A very "everyone is welcome" feel with no disturbances. Excellent dance music attracts most of the young to middle-age group of gay, lesbian, and bisexual people — as well as some of the college crowd.

▼ ⚤

BATHS/SAUNAS

Apollo Sauna Bath
1547 Barrington St., B3J 1Z4
PHONE: 423-6549

BOOKSHOPS/LIBRARIES

Entitlement — The Book Company
5675 Spring Garden Rd.
Lord Nelson Commercial Complex, B3J 1H1
PHONE: 420-0565, FAX: 420-3201
Toll-Free (from Atlantic provinces): 1-800-565-2665
A general bookstore with an extensive selection of fiction/non-fiction. Although there isn't a section for gay/lesbian issues, there are lots of books stocked on these subjects: everything from drama anthologies to queer Christian texts to cultural studies and life-styles. Mail orders are accepted.
♿ ▽ ⚥

Red Herring Co-op Books
1555 Granville St., B3J 1W7
PHONE: 422-5087
Alternative bookstore with a large selection on gay and lesbian issues and non-fiction/fiction. Also books on spirituality, feminist theory, and gay travel. Mail orders are accepted.
HOURS: Monday to Wednesday, Saturday 10:00 a.m. – 6:00 p.m.
Thursday and Friday 10:00 a.m. – 9:00 p.m.
Sunday 1:00 p.m. – 5:00 p.m.
PAYMENT: cash, personal and traveller's cheques, MasterCard, VISA
♿ ▼ ⚥

PUBLICATIONS

Wayves (formerly *Gaezette*)
P.O. Box 34090, Scotia Square B3J 3S1
The only gay and lesbian newspaper put out for the Atlantic provinces. Monthly.
▼ ⚣ ⚢

RESTAURANTS/CAFÉS

Of Course . . . A Café & Bistro
5657 Spring Garden Rd.
P.O. Box 140 Park Lane Mall, B3J 3R4
PHONE: 492-2229
A full-service café and bistro located in Park Lane Mall. The menu consists of great pastas, gourmet pizza, innovative salads, and much more. Fully licensed.
♿ ▼ ⚧

SERVICES

Gay and Lesbian Association of Nova Scotia (GALA)
2112 Gottingen St., B3K 3B3
PHONE: 423-2292, or 429-GALA for community-events line

Gayline
PHONE: 423-7129
HOURS: Thursday to Saturday 7:00 p.m. – 10:00 p.m.

Word Is Out
CKDU 97.5 FM
HOURS: Monday 7:00 p.m. – 8:00 p.m.

Lunenburg, Nova Scotia (902)

ACCOMMODATION/BED & BREAKFAST

Brook House
3 Old Blue Rocks Rd., B0J 2C0
PHONE: 634-3826
Brook House was built by a shipbuilder during the American Civil War. It is a stone's throw from the shipyard that produced the Bluenose and it overlooks the landing place of the original Lunenburg settlers. Two comfortable rooms with private baths. A substantial continental breakfast is served. Three cats in residence.
RATES: $45 to $55
PAYMENT: cash, traveller's cheques, MasterCard, VISA
▼ ⚥

Shelburne, Nova Scotia (902)

ACCOMMODATION/BED & BREAKFAST

The Toddle Inn Dining/Lodging & The Curiosity Shoppe
163 Water St., B0T 1W0
PHONE: 875-3229
For reservations call Check Inns at 1-800-565-0000
Toddle Inn is a Victorian inn offering period-decorated rooms and home cooking. Recommended as one of Canada's 50 best buys in *Where To Eat in Canada.* Side trips to secluded beaches and points of interest are planned. Reservations are recommended. Wheelchair accessibility only in the dining room and the Shoppe. Open from first Monday in April until December 24.
▼ ⚥

Wolfville, Nova Scotia (902)

ACCOMMODATION/BED & BREAKFAST

Tattingstone Inn
434 Main St., B0P 1X0
PHONE: 542-7696, FAX: 542-4427

VISITING *Prince Edward Island*

For visitor information:

Visitor Services
P.O. Box 940
Charlottetown, Prince Edward Island C1A 7M5
PHONE: 1-800-565-0267

Summer in Prince Edward Island is cool, but the weather can turn cold and wet in August. Winter is wet and cold, usually with strong winds, sometimes blowing with such force you may want to call for Auntie Em.

The Provincial Sales Tax is 10 percent, and the legal drinking age is 19.

GETTING AROUND PRINCE EDWARD ISLAND

To get to the island, you can take a ferry, or fly in direct. A fixed link to the mainland is currently under construction.

There is no local bus system in P.E.I., but there are taxis, and driving around the province is fairly easy to do.

GAY PLACES OF INTEREST

Prince Edward Island has no defined gay and lesbian community, and there are few places of interest specific to vacationing gays and lesbians. There are two bars where gays and lesbians hang out, but they are not defined as gay or lesbian bars.

In 1994, Charlottetown held its first Gay Pride March, consisting of about 100 participants. Gay Pride Day is usually held on the last Sunday in June.

ENTERTAINMENT

Prince Edward Island is virtually surrounded by beautiful beaches. It also has plenty of cycling and hiking trails, and many golfing facilities.

Cultural events are held year-round on Prince Edward Island.

During the first week of February, you can attend the Charlottetown Winter Carnival. It is Atlantic Canada's premier winter festival, with hockey tournaments, relay races, and other sporting activities.

The Confederation Centre Art Gallery and Museum in Charlottetown is open June to September from 10:00 a.m to 8:00 p.m. daily. For an admission of two dollars for adults, art lovers can view the many paintings, sculptures, drawings, and other art treasures on display.

CRUISING AREAS

The cruising areas in Prince Edward Island are not widely publicized. However, to meet gays and lesbians, you can visit Doc's Corner or the Island Rock Café, two bars in Charlottetown where gays and lesbians hang out. They are not specifically gay bars, so be careful who you're eyeing.

Charlottetown, Prince Edward Island (902)

ACCOMMODATION/BED & BREAKFAST

Charlottetown Hotel
P.O. Box 159, C1A 7K4
PHONE: 894-7371, FAX: 368-2178

BARS

Doc's Corner
185 Kent St., C1A 1P1
PHONE: 566-1069

Island Rock Café
132 Richmond St., C1A 1H9
PHONE: 892-2222
⚥

SERVICES

AIDS P.E.I. Community Support Group Inc.
199 Grafton St., C1A 1L2
Mailing address: P.O. Box 2762, C1A 8C4
PHONE/FAX: 566-2437
AIDS P.E.I. offers education and support services for PWA's, partners, family, and friends.
HOURS: Monday to Friday 9:00 a.m. – 5:00 p.m.
PAYMENT: cash, cheques
♿ ▽ ⚥

PEI Gay Phoneline
PHONE: 566-9733
HOURS: women: Wednesday 7:00 p.m. – 10:00 p.m.
men: Thursday 7:00 p.m. – 10:00 p.m.

Vernon Bridge, Prince Edward Island (902)

ACCOMMODATION/BED & BREAKFAST

Blair Hall
Vernon Bridge, P.E.I., COA 2EO
PHONE: 651-2202
Toll-Free: 1-800-268-7005
Situated on Orwell Bay, 15 minutes from Charlottetown.
Three-storey home full of many interesting antiques.
RATES: $45 to $50
PAYMENT: cash, traveller's cheques
▼ ⚥

Province of British Columbia

British Columbia entered Confederation in 1871. At that time, the population of the province was mostly of British descent. There is today, however, an ever-increasing number of people of Chinese and Japanese origin. Most of the population lives in the southwestern corner of the province.

British Columbia is Canada's most westerly province, and is flanked by the Rocky Mountains to the east, and the Pacific Ocean to the west.

Jane Rule, author of the classic lesbian love story *Desert of the Heart*, calls this beautiful province home.

The Provincial Sales Tax is 7 percent and the legal age for drinking is 19.

Burnaby, B.C. (604)

BOOKSHOPS/LIBRARIES

Imperial Books
4924 Imperial St., V5J 1C6
PHONE: 432-9940
The clean little dirty bookstore just east of Metrotown in Burnaby. We sell, trade, and buy back magazines, books, and videos.
HOURS: Monday to Thursday 11:00 a.m. – 7:00 p.m.
Friday 11:00 a.m. – 9:00 p.m.
Saturday 11:00 a.m. – 7:00 p.m.
Sunday 11:00 a.m. – 5:00 p.m.
PAYMENT: cash, MasterCard, VISA
♿ ▼ ⚦

Duncan, B.C. (604)

SERVICES

Island Gay/Lesbian Society of Duncan
PHONE: 748-7689

Kelowna, B.C. (604)

SERVICES

Okanagan Gay/Lesbian Organization
P.O. Box 711, Station A, V1Y 7P4
PHONE: 860-8555
HOURS: Daily 7:00 p.m. – 10:00 p.m.

Mt. Lehmann, B.C. (604)

ACCOMMODATION/BED & BREAKFAST

Rural Roots B&B
4939 Ross Rd., V4X 1Z3
PHONE: 856-2380, FAX: 857-2380
Pamper yourself. Affordable, luxurious country living, one hour's drive from Vancouver. Ten park-like acres, hot tub, sun decks, conservatory, and full breakfasts.
RATES: $40 single, $65 double
PAYMENT: cash, personal and traveller's cheques
▼ ⚣ ⚢

Nelson, B.C. (604)

SERVICES

West Kootenay Gay/Lesbian Referral Line
PHONE: 354-4297

Pender Island, B.C. (604)

ACCOMMODATION/BED & BREAKFAST

Eagle Ridge Gulf Island Getaway
RR#1 Pender
PHONE: 629-3692

Port Alberni, B.C. (604)

BOOKSHOPS/LIBRARIES

Curious Coho Books
4841 Johnston Rd., V9Y 5M2
PHONE: 724-2141, FAX: 723-1736
Good selection of non-explicit gay/lesbian magazines and small gay/lesbian book section.
HOURS: Monday to Wednesday, Saturday 9:30 a.m. – 6:00 p.m.
Thursday and Friday 9:30 a.m. – 9:00 p.m.
Sunday noon – 4:00 p.m.
PAYMENT: cash, traveller's cheques, MasterCard, VISA (soon to have INTERAC)
♿ ▼ ⚥

Prince George, B.C. (604)

ACCOMMODATION/BED & BREAKFAST

Hawthorne B&B
RR#4, Site 7, Comp 10, V2N 2J2
PHONE: 563-8299, FAX: 563-0899
Two guest rooms decorated with antiques and fine linens. Nice river views. Private outdoor hot tub, coffee service, exercise room, reading and music rooms.
RATES: $60 single, $70 double
PAYMENT: cash, traveller's cheques, MasterCard, VISA
▼ ⚦

SERVICES

GALA North
PHONE: 562-6253

Prince Rupert, B.C. (604)

SERVICES

Gay Info Line
PHONE: 627-8900

Revelstoke, B.C. (604)

SERVICES

Lothlorien
Box 8557, V0E 3G0

Salt Spring Island, B.C. (604)

ACCOMMODATION/BED & BREAKFAST

The Blue Ewe Bed & Breakfast
1207 Beddis Rd.
PHONE: 537-9344
(You can call collect)
Over five acres of privacy with forested paths, ponds, ocean, and mountain views. The hot tub is wonderful, the rooms first class, and the food is gourmet. Dogs, cats, sheep, goats, and the ducks are all friendly. Offering kayaking, dinner paddles to small islands, moonlight paddles, sea lion and seal tours, overnight tours, trail rides, and fishing trips.
PAYMENT: cash, personal and traveller's cheques, MasterCard, VISA
▼ ⚣ ⚢

Green Rose Farm Bed & Breakfast
346 Robinson Rd., V8K 1P7
PHONE: 537-9927
An authentic 1916 Salt Spring Island farm house, set amidst 17 acres of fields, orchards, and forest. Our guest rooms evoke the mood of old summer homes somewhere near the sea. Crisp, uncluttered spaces and, in the morning, a memorable breakfast inspired by the season.
PAYMENT: cash, MasterCard, VISA
▼ ⚥

Salt Spring Driftwood Gallery Bed & Brunch
1982 North End Rd., V8K 1C9
PHONE: 537-4137

Summerhill Guest House
209 Chu-An Dr., V8K 1H9
PHONE: 537-2727, FAX: 537-4301
At the water's edge on magnificent Salt Spring Island. Beautifully appointed guest rooms overlook either the ocean or rolling meadows. All rooms have private bath. Swim at nearby beaches or explore numerous walking, hiking, and cycling trails. Sail, canoe, or kayak the coastline. Browse the shops and galleries in the village. In summer, escape with a book to the sun-drenched

decks. In winter, relax by the fire in the tranquil sitting room. Good ferry and float plane connections from Vancouver.

RATES: $70 to $95, which includes a delicious full breakfast.

PAYMENT: cash, traveller's cheques, MasterCard, VISA

▼ ⚤

Sunnyside Up B&B

120 Andrew Place, Fulford Harbour, V8K 1X3

PHONE: 653-4889

A rustic, restful haven tucked away on six wooded acres, overlooking the ocean. Country breakfasts, guided hiking trails, and stargazing from a jacuzzi.

RATES: $70 single (off season: $60)
$85 double (off season: $75)

PAYMENT: cash, traveller's cheques, MasterCard, VISA

♿ ▼ ⚤

Tofino, B.C. (604)

ACCOMMODATION/BED & BREAKFAST

The West Wind Guest House

1321 Pacific Rim Hwy, V0R 2Z0

PHONE: 725-2224

⚣ ⚢

VANCOUVER: *A Brief Description*

Vancouver, known as Canada's "lotus-land," is Canada's third-largest and fastest growing city. It is culturally diverse, boasts a large and exciting gay and lesbian community, and is regarded as being one of the world's most beautiful cities.

VISITING VANCOUVER

For visitor information:

Greater Vancouver CB
5 Bentall Ctr., 555 Burrard St., Vancouver, British Columbia V7X 1M7
PHONE: (604) 682-2222

For gay visitor information:
PHONE: (604) 684-6869

Winters tend to be mild, and summers are cool. The temperate climate means it seldom snows in winter, but it more than makes up for it in rain. Always take your umbrella.

GETTING AROUND VANCOUVER

Vancouver International Airport is a bustling, modern facility served by Canadian Airlines International (whose headquarters is in Vancouver), Air Canada, and several other major carriers. Vancouver is also the western terminus of Via Rail Canada. Vancouver's metropolitan area has an efficient and integrated public transit system, including many diesel and trolley bus routes, the Sky Train (an elevated light rail vehicle running underground in the city core), and the Sea Bus (a hovercraft service in Burrard Inlet connecting downtown Vancouver to North Vancouver). Frequent bus service is available to the B.C. Ferries (there are many "ferries" in B.C.), to the Horseshoe Bay ferries, to Nanaimo on Vancouver Island, to the Tsawassen ferries, to Swarz Bay (for Victoria), and to the Gulf Islands.

GAY PLACES OF INTEREST

In the West End of Vancouver, near English Bay Beach and Stanley Park, is the gay area of town. There are many gay and lesbian bars, restaurants, and shopping establishments found here, located mostly around Davie Street.

In an area known as "The Drive," which is located on Commerical Drive in the city's east end, you will find the main lesbian drag. When here, be sure to visit The Lotus Club, the lesbian community's oldest dyke bar.

Vancouver's Gay Pride Day is celebrated on the first Monday of August, complete with parade, concert in the park, and a beer garden. Call the local gayline for more information.

ENTERTAINMENT

Vancouver's cultural life is rich and diverse. Vancouver has a planetarium and a symphony orchestra performing in the restored Orpheum Theatre. The Opera Association and Playhouse Theatre both use the Queen Elizabeth Theatre. There are many other drama and dance groups.

Vancouver's magnificent aquarium sits in Stanley Park, a huge wilderness area near downtown and the West End (where there is a concentration of lesbian/gay resources).

The B.C. Lions football team plays at B.C. Place, Canada's first covered stadium.

CRUISING AREAS

Vancouver has many cruising areas. Stanley Park offers plenty of scope for cyclists, joggers, and those gay men out for an evening's "cruise." Another favourite cruising spot is Wreck Beach, stretching for a considerable distance at the base of the cliffs bordering the University of British Columbia. The beach is accessible by a steep climb down to an area where straights are "letting it all hang out" to the left, and gays are similarly in the buff to the right. Remember once you're here to head in the "right" direction.

Other cruising areas include Denman Street, Robson Street, Davie Street, and the "Fruit Loop" parking lot at the beach.

Vancouver, B.C. (604)

ACCOMMODATION/BED & BREAKFAST

The Albion Guest House
592 West 19th Ave., V5Z 1W6
PHONE: 873-2287, FAX: 879-5682
Toll-Free: feel free to call collect
Features fabulous beds, a fireplace, and a romantic hot tub. A private bathroom is available. Close to everything. Bikes for loan.
RATES: $85 to $120 summer,
$48 to $90 winter
PAYMENT: cash, personal and traveller's cheques, MasterCard, VISA
▼ ⚣ ⚢

Buchan Hotel
1906 Haro St., V6G 1H7
FAX: 685-5367
Toll-Free: 1-800-668-6654

Colibri Bed & Breakfast
1101 Thurlow St., V6E 1W9
PHONE: 689-5100, FAX: 682-3925
Steps from all downtown action. Extraordinary hospitality in an extraordinary atmosphere. This address was previously Gables Guest House.
RATES: $55 to $120 per night
PAYMENT: cash, traveller's cheques, American Express, MasterCard, VISA
▼ ⚥

Columbia Cottage
205 West 14th Ave., V5Y 1X2
PHONE: 874-5327, FAX: 879-4547
A 1920s Tudor home located seven minutes from downtown in beautiful heritage area. All rooms come with private bath and suite, decorated with original artwork. Feather beds, gowns in rooms, home-baked treats and wonderful gourmet breakfasts by resident chef.
HOURS: Daily 8:00 a.m. – 10:00 p.m.
PAYMENT: personal and traveller's cheques, MasterCard, VISA
▽ ⚥

Dufferin Hotel
900 Seymour St., V6B 3L9
PHONE: 683-4251
FAX: 683-0611
Also holds three bars: Avenue Lounge, Back Alley, and Forge.
⚥

Heritage House Hotel
455 Abbott St., V6B 2L2
PHONE: 685-7777
Vintage and unique 110-room hotel in downtown Vancouver, adjacent to Chinatown, Gastown, bus lines, and Skytrain. Also the home of three bars: Chuck's Pub, Uncle Charlie's Lounge, and The Lotus (See BARS heading).
PAYMENT: cash, MasterCard, VISA
♿ ▼ ⚥

Joy of Roses B&B
4040 Ontario St., V5V 3G5
PHONE: 874-2082, FAX: 874-4099
Located in an old established residential area of Vancouver called Little Mountain. A self-contained ground-floor suite with sliding glass doors leading to a secluded, tranquil garden of fragrant roses. Laundry facilities available at no extra cost. On arrival, guests will find a small bottle of wine and homemade cookies waiting for them. Breakfast is included.
RATES: $80/night for two people, $70/night for one person
10% discount for six nights or longer
PAYMENT: cash, Canadian traveller's cheques
▽

Nelson House Bed & Breakfast
977 Broughton St., V6G 2A4
PHONE: 684-9793
Great downtown location. Fireplaces, decks, and character galore. Five spacious rooms in renovated Edwardian. One jacuzzi ensuite, two shared baths, and washbasins in rooms. Springer spaniel stress relief and super break-

fasts. David, O'Neal, Dorothy, and "Sam" will welcome you to Vancouver.
PAYMENT: cash, traveller's cheques, MasterCard, VISA
▼ ⚤

Papa's Place, Royal Hotel and Pub
1025 Granville St., V6Z 1L4
PHONE: 685-5335, FAX: 685-5351
Live entertainment Wednesday to Sunday. Located in downtown Vancouver.
RATES: Quoted on request
HOURS: Daily 10:00 a.m. – 11:00 p.m.
♿ ▽ ⚣ ⚢

Royal Hotel
1025 Granville St., V6Z 1L4
PHONE: 685-5335, FAX: 685-5351
⚤

Stay in Touch Guesthouse
PHONE: 681-2246
For women only. Downtown Vancouver. Phone for reservation and information. Queen-size bed, sauna, jacuzzi, and colour TV. Private balcony and washroom. Two weeks advance notice. Closed for the winter months.
RATES: $75
⚢

West End Guest House
1362 Haro St., V6E 1G2
PHONE: 681-2889, FAX: 688-8812
Centrally located for restaurants, tourist venues, Stanley Park, and within walking distance of bars. Turn-of-the-century house, lots of antiques and charm, colour TV, private baths, free parking, and bikes for loan.
HOURS: Daily 7:00 a.m. – 10:00 p.m.
PAYMENT: personal and traveller's cheques, American Express, Discover, MasterCard, VISA
▼ ⚥

BARS

Bottom Line
1082 Granville St., V6Z 1L5
PHONE: 688-1333
⚣ ⚢

Celebrities Cabaret

1022 Davie St., V6E 1M3

PHONE: 689-3180

Vancouver's largest and busiest gay night club. Sunday nights are "country" line-dancing lessons and two-steps.

[*Editor's note*: Sunday Nights are more lesbian.]

HOURS: Monday to Saturday 9:00 p.m. – 2:00 a.m.
Sunday 7:00 p.m. – midnight

PAYMENT: cash, VISA

♿ ▼ ⚣ ⚢ ⚤

Chuck's Pub/Uncle Charlie's Lounge/The Lotus

c/o Heritage House Hotel

455 Abbott St., V6B 2L2

Chuck's Pub has a male orientation and the cabaret (The Lotus) is women-only on Friday nights.

See the Heritage House Hotel under ACCOMMODATION/BED & BREAKFAST heading for further details.

⚣ ⚢ ⚤

Denman Station

860 Denman St., V6G 2L8

PHONE: 669-3448

⚣ ⚢

Fly Girl/Jet Boy
PHONE: Little Sister's 699-1753
[*Editor's note*: At time of publication, Fly Girl is a moving women's dance bar on some Saturday nights, and Jet Boy is a moving gay male dance bar on some Sunday nights. Often held at Studio 16, 1545 West 7th.]

Forge Tavern
c/o Dufferin Pub
900 Seymour St., V6B 3L9
PHONE: 683-4251

Graceland
1250 Richards St., V6B 3G2
PHONE: 688-2648, FAX: 688-7548
Graceland — except for sex, there is nothing better. Drink, dance, have a good time.
[*Editor's note*: Holds gay dances on Sunday nights.]
HOURS: Daily 9:00 p.m. – 2:00 a.m.
PAYMENT: cash, MasterCard, VISA
♿ ▽ ⚥

Ms. T's
339 West Pender St., V6B 1T3
PHONE: 682-8096
⚢

Numbers Cabaret
1042 Davie St., V6E 1M3
PHONE: 685-4077, FAX: 685-8025
Five levels on two floors. Dance floor, pool tables, and darts. Mostly gay male.
HOURS: Monday to Saturday 8:00 p.m. – 2:00 a.m.
Sunday 8:00 p.m. – midnight
PAYMENT: cash, traveller's cheques
▼ ⚣ ⚢

✓**Odyssey**
1251 Howe St., V6Z 1R3
PHONE: 689-5256, FAX: 689-5410
One of Vancouver's hottest gay dance floors, featuring a patio bar and a naked-or-not shower. Go-go platforms and cage round off the techno/disco beats. The hottest of men dance down. Definitely a gay men's place to be seen and enjoyed.

HOURS: Monday to Saturday 9:00 p.m. – 2:00 a.m.
Sunday 9:00 p.m. – midnight
PAYMENT: cash, VISA
♿ ▼ ⚣ ⚢

Papa's Place, Royal Hotel and Pub
1025 Granville St., V6Z 1L4
(See listing under ACCOMMODATION/BED & BREAKFAST.)

The Riley T
1661 Granville St., V6Z 1N3
PHONE: 684-3666
No host bar and restaurant. An alternative affair from 5:00 p.m. on the first and third Sunday of the month.
⚣

The Shaggy Horse
818 Richards St., V6B 3A7
PHONE: 688-2923
[*Editor's note*: Vancouver's oldest gay bar, but exercise some caution here because it is becoming more straight.]
⚣

Underground
1082 Granville St., V6Z 1L5
(rear entrance)
Dance and cruise bar.
⚣

BATHS/SAUNAS

Club Vancouver
339 West Pender St., V6B 1T3
PHONE: 681-5719
Located in the downtown area near major hotels, entertainment, and gay clubs. Universal gym, tanning room, TV lounge, steam room, snack bar, games room, single and double rooms, in and out privileges extended to visitors.
HOURS: Daily 24 hours
▼ ⚣

F212° Steam

971 Richards St., V6B 3B6
PHONE: 689-9719
Vancouver's largest bath. Heated floors, two steam rooms, a jacuzzi tub, and two television/video lounges.
PAYMENT: cash, traveller's cheques, VISA
▼ ⚣

Nuwest Steam Bath

533 Front St., New Westminster, V3L 1A4
PHONE: 526-2913

Richards Street Service Club

1169 Richards St., V6B 3E7
PHONE: 684-6010

BOOKSHOPS/LIBRARIES

Book Mantle

1002 Commercial Dr., V5L 3W9
PHONE: 253-1099

Duthie's Books

919 Robson St., V6Z 1A5
PHONE: 684-4496

✓Little Sister's Book & Art Emporium

1221 Thurlow St., V6E 1X4
PHONE: 669-1753, FAX: 685-0252
Toll-free: 1-800-567-1662
Little Sister's is western Canada's gay/lesbian bookstore. Carries a wide range of books and other materials, so drop by and check them out. Catalogue available and mail orders accepted.
HOURS: Daily 10:00 a.m. – 11:00 p.m.
PAYMENT: cash, traveller's cheques, Debit Cards, American Express, MasterCard, VISA
▼ ⚣ ⚢

Octopus Books
1146 Commercial Dr., V5L 3X2
PHONE: 253-0913
A progressive bookstore, specializing in magazines and alternative new and used books.
HOURS: Monday to Sunday 10:00 a.m. – 6:00 p.m.
PAYMENT: cash, personal and traveller's cheques, MasterCard, VISA
♿ ▽ ⚧

Spartacus Books
311 West Hastings St., V5L 2K8
PHONE: 688-6138
Spartacus Books is a non-profit organization that was founded as a Non-Sectarian Socialist Education Society. Currently, Spartacus carries a broad range of new books and periodicals in such "progressive"/left/social movement areas as: gay/lesbian studies, native studies, "race" studies, feminism, ecology, philosophy, politics, fiction, etc. Mail orders accepted.
▽ ⚧

Vancouver Women's Bookstore
315 Cambie St., V6B 2N4
PHONE: 684-0523
Toll-free: 1-800-610-6222
A non-profit workers' co-op and feminist bookstore with music, periodicals, children's books, and literature by, for, and about women. Mail orders accepted and catalogue available.
HOURS: Monday to Saturday 10:00 a.m. – 6:00 p.m.
PAYMENT: cash, personal and traveller's cheques, MasterCard, VISA
▽ ⚧ ♀

Women in Print
3566 West 4th Ave., V6R 1N8
PHONE: 732-4128
FAX: 732-4129
Full range of feminist books including strong lesbian section. Magazines, cards, t-shirts, videos, and an efficient special order service.
HOURS: Monday to Saturday 10:00 a.m. – 6:00 p.m.
Sunday noon – 5:00 p.m.
PAYMENT: cash, personal and traveller's cheques, MasterCard, VISA
♿ ▼ ⚧

CHURCHES/RELIGIOUS ORGANIZATIONS

Dignity/Integrity
PHONE: 432-1230

Christ Alive Metropolitan Community Church
3214 West 10th Ave., V6B 4B2
PHONE: 739-7959
HOURS: Meets Sundays at 7:15 p.m.
♿ ▼ ⚧

Liberty Community Church
1401 Comox St., V6G 1N9
PHONE: 254-0082
HOURS: Sunday at 6:30 p.m. at St. John's United Church.

HEALTH CLUBS

Harbour Relaxation
203 – 1107 Homer St., V6B 2Y1
PHONE: 687-1020
Massage services for a healthy life-style. Serving Vancouver and the lower mainland for men and women.
HOURS: Monday to Sunday 11:00 a.m. – 1:00 a.m.
PAYMENT: cash, American Express
♿ ▼ ⚧

YMCA
955 Burrard St., V6Z 1Y2
PHONE: 681-0221

PUBLICATIONS

Angles
1170 Bute St., V6E 1Z6
PHONE: 688-0265, FAX: 688-5405
The magazine of Vancouver's lesbian, gay, and bisexual communities. A monthly magazine-style newspaper which offers a lesbian, gay, and/or bisexual perspective on contemporary events, politics, arts, and entertainment.

Angles is volunteer-based and has been committed to the goals of gay, lesbian, and bisexual liberation for more than 10 years.
HOURS: Monday to Friday noon-2:00 p.m.
Wednesday 6:00 p.m. – 9:00 p.m.
▼ ⚣ ⚢

Lezzie Smut
Hey Grrrlz! Productions
Box 364, 1027 Davie St., V6E 4L2
⚢

Kinesis
301 – 1720 Grant St., V5L 2Y6
PHONE: 255-5499, FAX: 255-5511
♀

XTRA West Newspaper
501 – 1033 Davie St., V6E 1M5
PHONE: 684-9696, FAX: 684-9697
Other Numbers: Tel-A-Guide 688-WEST (24-hour touch-tone guide to Vancouver's gay & lesbian community)
XTC (*XTRA West*'s Talking Classifieds) 257-5555 (24-hour telephone dating for both gay men and lesbians)
Vancouver's gay/lesbian biweekly covering news, arts, and entertainment.
HOURS: Monday to Friday 9:00 a.m. – 5:00 p.m.
PAYMENT: cash, personal cheques, MasterCard, VISA
♿ ▼ ⚣ ⚢

RESTAURANTS/CAFÉS

Café Luxy
1235 Davie St., V6E 1N4
PHONE: 681-9976

Café S'il Vous Plait
500 Robson St., V6B 2B7
PHONE: 688-7216

Clearwater Café
1030 Denman St., V6G 2M6
PHONE: 688-6264, FAX: 689-1968

Gourmet natural-foods restaurant featuring fine vegetarian cuisine, great music, and friendly, relaxed atmosphere.

HOURS: Monday to Friday 11:30 a.m. – 10:00 or 11:00 p.m.
Weekends and holidays 10:00 a.m. – 10:00 or 11:00 p.m.

PAYMENT: cash, traveller's cheques, MasterCard, VISA

♿ ▼ ⚥

Dakoda's Coffee House

1602 Yew St., Kitsilano V6K 3E7

PHONE: 730-9266, FAX: 730-9277

Serves dessert, pastries, sandwiches, light lunches, and breakfast goodies.

HOURS: Monday to Friday 7:00 a.m. – 11:00 p.m.
Saturday and Sunday 8:00 a.m. – 11:00 p.m.

PAYMENT: cash, MasterCard, VISA

♿ ▽ ⚥

Delilah's

1906 Haro St., V6G 1H7

PHONE: 687-3424

Doll & Penny's Diner

1167 Davie St., V6E 1N2

PHONE: 685-3417

This is a uniquely zany venue and is not for those who take fun too seriously! Situated in downtown Vancouver for over 20 years, it is famous as an after-club spot with funky artwork and staff. West-coast food — comprehensive selection of appetizers, burgers, sandwiches, pastas, and entrees.

♿ ▽ ⚥

The Edge Café

1148 Davie St., V6E 1N1

PHONE: 689-4742

Elbow Room Café

720 Jervis, V6E 2A8

PHONE: 685-3628, FAX: 270-0647

Famous for its breakfasts, great menu, good prices, excellent food, and the abuse is free. This establishment has won awards for its breakfast service.

HOURS: Monday to Friday 7:30 a.m. – 3:30 p.m.
Weekends 8:30 a.m. – 3:30 p.m.

PAYMENT: cash, traveller's cheques, MasterCard, VISA

▼ ⚥

Espressohead Coffee House
1945 Cornwall Ave., V6J 1C8
PHONE: 739-1069, FAX: 732-8820
Express yourself with a fabulous latte, a mocha, or a cappuccino. Also a delectable selection of desserts.
HOURS: Sunday to Thursday 7:00 a.m. – midnight
Friday and Saturday 7:00 a.m. – 1:00 a.m.
PAYMENT: cash, traveller's cheques
♿ ▽ ⚥

Flying Wedge Pizza Co.
1175 Robson St., V6E 1B5
PHONE: 681-1233

Hamburger Mary's
1202 Davie St., V6E 1M3
PHONE: 687-1293

Harry's
1716 Charles St., V5L 2T5
PHONE: 253-1789

La Di Da Restaurant and Catering
1030 Davie St., V6E 1M3
PHONE: 689-3688, FAX: 688-0173
International gourmet dining in a cozy and relaxed atmosphere at reasonable cost. Nightly live piano entertainment. Catering for all occasions.
HOURS: Daily 11:00 a.m. – midnight
PAYMENT: cash, traveller's cheques, MasterCard, VISA
♿ ▼ ⚥

La Quena
1111 Commercial Dr., V5L 3X3
PHONE: 251-6626
All volunteer-run, La Quena offers low-cost vegetarian food and a cultural/political venue for Vancouver's progressive community.
⚥

O-Tooz Energy Bar
1068 Davie St., V6E 1M3
PHONE: 689-0208

The Second Cup
103 – 1184 Denman St., V6G 2M9
PHONE: 669-2068
The best coffee and tea in town, including espresso, caffè latte, and cappuccino.
♿ ▽ ⚥

Takis' Taverna
1106 Davie St., V6E 1N1
PHONE: 682-1336

RETAIL

Antix
1072 Davie St., V6E 1M3
PHONE: 682-4161

Applause Videos
2595 Commercial Dr., V5N 4C1
PHONE: 874-3133

D&R Clothing Etc.
1112 Davie St., V6Z 1N1
PHONE: 687-0937, FAX: 685-1553
The latest in men's activewear, clubwear, underwear, socks, jewellery, and sunglasses. Locally made shirts and vests. Lots of tight-fitting goods.
♿ ▼ ⚥

Mack's Leather Inc.
1043 Granville St., V6Z 1C4
PHONE: 688-6225
Exotic & erotic leathers — custom or ready-made; body piercing by Canada's most experienced body piercer. Catalogue available.
♿ ▽ ⚥

Next! BodyPiercing
1068 Granville St., V6Z 1A1
PHONE: 684-6398

Pleasure Chest
1155 Davie St., V6E 1N2
PHONE: 683-2468
Peep Shows — 24 hours

Return to Sender
1076 Davie St., V6E 1M3
PHONE: 683-6363

State of Mind
1100 Davie St., V6E 1N1
PHONE: 682-7116
Clothing and jewellery on the cutting edge of fashion for men and women.
HOURS: Monday to Saturday 10:00 a.m. – 7:00 p.m.
Sunday noon – 5:00 p.m.
PAYMENT: cash, traveller's cheques, Debit Card, American Express, VISA
♿ ▼ ⚤

Top Drawers Apparel Inc.
115 – 1030 Denman St. V6G 2M6
PHONE: 684-4861
Top Drawers specializes in fashion underwear, loungewear, activewear, swimwear, and accessories — all for men.
HOURS: Saturday to Wednesday 10:00 a.m. – 6:00 p.m.
Thursday and Friday 10:00 a.m. – 9:00 p.m.
Sunday noon – 5:00 p.m.
PAYMENT: cash, traveller's cheques, American Express, MasterCard, VISA
♿ ▼ ⚤

Transitions Boutique/Rainbow's End
573 East Hastings St., V6A 1P9
PHONE: 254-6280

Videomatica Sales Ltd./Videomatica Rentals Ltd.
Sales: 1859 West 4th Ave., V6J 1M4
Rentals: 1855 West 4th Ave., V6J 1M4
PHONE: (Sales) 734-5752, (Rentals) 734-0411, FAX: 734-8867
Toll-free: 1-800-665-1469
Canada's best source for video and laser disc since 1983. Gay interest catalogue available (non-XXX), movies from $19.99 and up. For mail order call the toll-free number.
HOURS: Sales: Monday to Saturday 10:00 a.m. – 6:00 p.m.
Friday 10:00 a.m. – 7:00 p.m., Sunday noon – 5:00 p.m.
Rentals: Daily 10:00 a.m. – 10:00 p.m.
Friday and Saturday until 11:00 p.m.
PAYMENT: cash, personal and traveller's cheques, MasterCard, VISA
♿ ▼ ⚤

SERVICES

Gay & Lesbian Centre of Vancouver
1170 Bute St., V6E 1Z6
PHONE: 684-5307, FAX: 688-5405
Provides community services to Metro Vancouver. Services include a helpline, library, health clinic, legal clinic, professional counselling, and other groups.
HOURS: Daily 10:00 a.m. – 10:00 p.m.
PAYMENT: cash, personal cheques, MasterCard, VISA
▼ ⚣ ⚢

Persons With AIDS Society of British Columbia
1107 Seymour St., V6B 5S8
PHONE: 681-2122, FAX: 893-2251

Vancouver Lesbian Connection
876 Commercial Dr., V5L 3W6
PHONE: 254-8458, FAX: 254-8115
Canada's largest operating lesbian centre is one of the services offered by the Vancouver Lesbian Connection. A variety of support groups, political and human rights action groups, and lesbian education services. All lesbians are welcome.
HOURS: Tuesday and Thursday noon-7:00 p.m.
Saturday noon – 5:00 p.m.
▼ ⚢

TRAVEL/TOURS

S&S Travel Broker
104 – 8611 Ackroyd Rd., Richmond V6X 3P4
PHONE: 270-0647
Provides a variety of services. Specializing in cruises and tour companies. The focus is on the client and not an agency or wholesaler, therefore prices are lower.
▼ ⚥

Team Travel
1800 – 1140 West Pender St., V6E 4G1
PHONE: 688-9655, FAX: 688-0902
Toll-free: 1-800-663-0208

Travel management company serving the gay and lesbian community and offering travel packages, airline tickets, hotel reservations, as well as organizing group tours and sport tours for the community. A member of the IGTA.
♿ ▽ ⚧

Uniglobe Specialty Travel/Super Natural Adventure Tours
Main floor, 626 West Pender St., V6B 1V9
PHONE: 688-8816, FAX: 688-3317
Toll-free: 1-800-263-1600
A full-service travel agency with an in-house soft-adventure tour operator specializing in the Pacific Northwest. A vacation specialist can book any destinations worldwide, gay or non-gay.
HOURS: Monday to Friday 8:30 a.m. – 5:30 p.m.
PAYMENT: cash, personal and traveller's cheques, American Express, MasterCard, VISA
♿ ▽ ⚧

OTHER

Our Place
1046 Davie St., V6E 1M3
PHONE: 682-8368
Pool hall.
⚧

Sappho Lesbian Witchcamp
P.O. Box 21510, 1850 Commercial Dr., V5N 4A0
PHONE: 253-7189
Annual summer camp for lesbians. This year from June 25 to 30.
⚢

Sounds & Furies Productions
P.O. Box 21510, 1850 Commercial Dr., V5N 4A0
PHONE: 253-7189
Events by and for lesbians. Contact Pat Hogan, Producer.
⚢

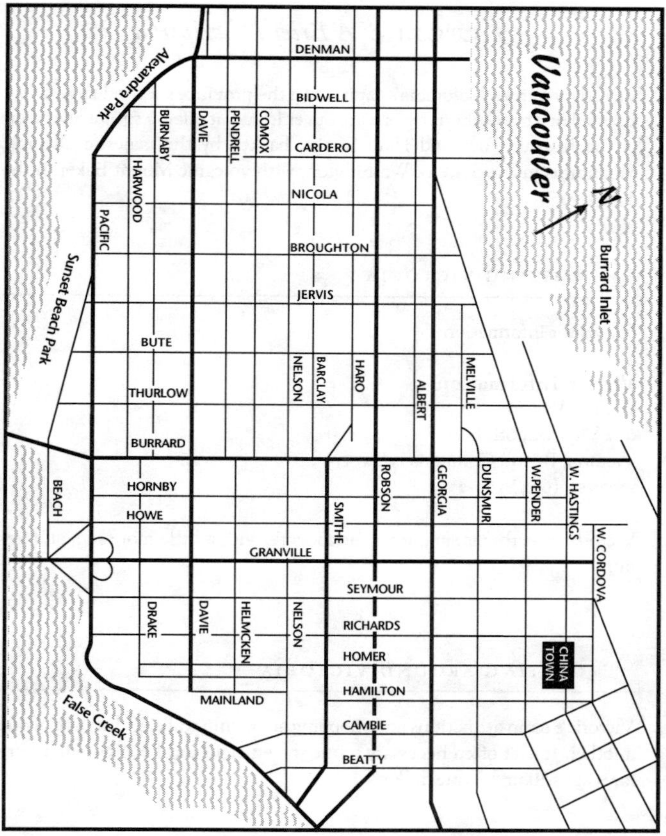
Vancouver
N
Burrard Inlet
Alexandra Park
Sunset Beach Park
False Creek
DENMAN
BIDWELL
CARDERO
NICOLA
BROUGHTON
JERVIS
BUTE
THURLOW
BURRARD
HORNBY
HOWE
GRANVILLE
SEYMOUR
RICHARDS
HOMER
HAMILTON
CAMBIE
BEATTY
MAINLAND
BURNABY
HARWOOD
PACIFIC
DAVIE
PENDRELL
COMOX
NELSON
BARCLAY
HARO
ALBERT
MELVILLE
ROBSON
GEORGIA
DUNSMUR
W.PENDER
W. HASTINGS
W. CORDOVA
SMITHE
BEACH
DRAKE
DAVIE
HELMCKEN
NELSON
CHINA TOWN

VICTORIA: *A Brief Description*

Victoria is British Columbia's capital and the province's second largest city. Located on the southern tip of Vancouver Island, it offers a spectacular view of the Juan de Fuca and Haro Straits, backed by the majestic Olympic Mountains in the State of Washington, with volcanic Mount Baker in the distance.

VISITING VICTORIA

For visitor information:

Visitor Information
Greater Victoria VCB
612 View St., 6th floor
Victoria, British Columbia V8W 1J5
PHONE: (604) 382-2160

Victoria's weather is similar to Vancouver's, with a little more sun, and less rain.

GETTING AROUND VICTORIA

Victoria's main attractions and shopping are within walking distance of one another. It isn't often necessary to use the efficient local bus system, where fares are still under one dollar.

GAY PLACES OF INTEREST/ENTERTAINMENT

Victoria's Buchart Gardens are a not-to-be-missed attraction, arguably the richest botanical preserve in the country. Cruising occurs here, too, but it is as discreet as the Gardens themselves. The Provincial Museum offers a unique glimpse of aboriginal artifacts, featuring totem poles and a recreated street from an earlier "Victorian" era.

CRUISING AREAS

Near the totem pole at the entrance to one of the pathways at Beacon Hill Park lies a good cruising area, with next to no police harassment.

Ten minutes outside of Victoria is Thetis Lake Park, and although the gay area is hard to find, it's well worth it. The Thetis Lake Park cruising area is found near a hidden exit, called Highland Road. At the end of this road, you'll find a large pile of rocks, and this area is known affectionately as "Blowjob Hill." The southern end of Beacon Hill Park along the seacoast also offers some good cruising.

The Empress Hotel, one of Canada's great railroad hotels, is a wonderful place to "take tea."

Victoria, B.C. (604)

ACCOMMODATION/BED & BREAKFAST

Advena Guesthouse
277 Durrance Rd., V8X 4M6
PHONE: 652-8132

The Black Hills Guest House for Women
4470 Leefield Rd., RR#1, V9B 5T7
PHONE: 478-9648
PAYMENT: cash, personal cheque
▼ ⚢

Claddagh House
1761 Lee Ave., V8R 4W7
PHONE: 370-2816
You can be assured of tasteful surroundings, music in your ears, incredible breakfasts, and hearty conversation with your Irish hosts in this 1913 heritage home. Step back from the pressures of everyday life and give yourself up to the relaxation and charm of a wholesome B&B experience. You might choose to enhance your experience with the "Island Escape" package, or a massage or reflexology treatment. Open year-round.
RATES: $55 to $85
PAYMENT: cash, traveller's cheques, MasterCard, VISA
▽ ♀ ⚤

Desjardins Guesthouse
1624 Chambers St., V8T 3J9
PHONE: 480-1560
Two dykes with three cats invite you to share our home and gardens. Send for a free brochure. Ici on parle français. Please phone ahead for reservations.
RATES: $50 per night. Breakfast included.
PAYMENT: cash, traveller's cheques
▼ ⚢

IFANWEN B&B
44 Simcoe St., V8V 1K2
PHONE: 384-3717
Cheerfully decorated, large room with queen-size bed and single hide-a-bed. Easy walk to waterfront and city centre. Featuring a full breakfast and a secret garden. Seasonal May through September.
RATES: $65 double
PAYMENT: cash
▼ ⚣ ⚢

Lavender Link Accommodations
136 Medana St., V8V 2H5
PHONE: 380-7098
Enjoy comfort in a tastefully renovated 1912 character home only minutes from the Inner Harbour and downtown and two blocks from the ocean. Shiatsu/kayaking can be arranged.

RATES: $65 to $75 double, including breakfast
$15 for each extra person
PAYMENT: cash, personal and traveller's cheques
▼ ⚣ ⚢

Oak Bay Guest House
1052 Newport Ave., V8S 5E3
PHONE: 598-3812

Pines Bed & Breakfast
3932 Quadra St., V8X 1J4
PHONE: 381-2750
Friendly atmosphere and home-cooked breakfasts. Ten minutes to downtown and 20 minutes to Buchart Gardens on bus line. Pick-up at airport or bus.
RATES: $40 double ($50 off season)
$35 single ($45 off season)
PAYMENT: cash, traveller's cheques
▼ ⚤

The Weekender Bed & Breakfast
10 Eberts St., V8S 5L6
PHONE: 389-1688
A seaside B&B located steps to the ocean along Victoria's scenic drive. A short distance to Beacon Hill Park, shopping, restaurants, night life, and most tourist atttractions. All guest rooms are spacious and have ensuite bathrooms.
⚣ ⚢

BARS

BJ's Lounge
642 Johnson St., V8W 1M6
PHONE/FAX: 388-0505
Video/piano lounge, live entertainment on weekends, a pool table, darts, and a friendly, relaxed atmosphere.
HOURS: Daily noon – 1:00 a.m.
PAYMENT: cash, traveller's cheques, INTERAC, MasterCard, VISA
♿ ▼ ⚣ ⚢

Rumors Cabaret
1325 Government St., V8W 1Y9
PHONE: 385-0566, FAX: 595-5125
High-energy night club with a quiet room.
HOURS: Monday to Saturday 9:00 p.m. – 2:00 a.m.
Sunday 9:00 p.m. – midnight
PAYMENT: cash, traveller's cheques, American Express, MasterCard, VISA
▼ ⚣ ⚢

BATHS/SAUNAS

Steam Works
582 Johnson St., V8W 1M3
PHONE: 383-6623
Sauna, pool table, and two video areas. Twenty-four rooms in all. Ask about lockers, rooms, or six-month memberships.
⚣

BOOKSHOPS/LIBRARIES

Everywomans Books
635 Johnson St., V8W 1M7
PHONE: 388-9411
The year 1995 marks this feminist bookstore's 20th anniversary. Run by a volunteer collective, the store carries books and sidelines, by, for, and about women, with a large lesbian stock. Mail orders accepted.
HOURS: Monday to Saturday 10:30 a.m. – 5:30 p.m.
PAYMENT: cash, personal and traveller's cheques, gift certificates, MasterCard, VISA
♿ ▽ ⚢ ♀

HEALTH CLUBS

Island Bodyworks
340 Irving Rd., V8S 4A2
PHONE: 370-2998
Esalen-certified massage practitioner. Deluxe studio and a whirlpool available.
▼ ⚥

RESTAURANTS/CAFÉS

Red Mango Market & Café
1725 Quadra St., V8W 2L7
PHONE: 385-2827

SERVICES

AIDS Vancouver Island
304 – 733 Johnson St., V8W 3C7
PHONE: 384-4554
HOURS: Monday to Friday 8:30 p.m. – 4:30 p.m.

Victoria Gayline
Box 695, Station E, V8V 2P9
PHONE: 598-4900
HOURS: Daily 6:30 p.m. – 10:30 p.m. (or whenever staff available)
[*Editor's note*: Never seems to be staffed. Machine will give you brief information on Hot Flashes Women's Café (monthly meeting), the bar Rumors, the Garden Baths, BJ's Lounge, and MCC.]

Whistler, B.C. (604)

ACCOMMODATION/BED & BREAKFAST

Coast Mountain Lodge
P.O. Box 1370, 7406 Ambassador Cres., V0N 1B0
PHONE: 938-1280, FAX: 938-1250
Luxury mountain chalet at one of North America's favourite ski resorts — Whistler. Relax and enjoy the company of fellow gays and lesbians in this perfect mountain setting. Great views, fireplace, and hot tub.
RATES: $50 to $100 summer
$100 to $150 winter
PAYMENT: cash, personal and traveller's cheques, MasterCard, VISA
▼ ⚣ ⚢

TRAVEL/TOURS

Whistler Gay Ski Week
Out On The Slopes Productions
P.O. Box 1370, VON 1BO
PHONE: 938-0772, FAX: 938-1250
Whistler gay and lesbian ski week. Join gays and lesbians from around the world for a week of skiing and fun at North America's best-rated resort. An annual event held the second week of February (in 1996 it will be held February 4 – 11).
PAYMENT: cash, personal and traveller's cheques, MasterCard, VISA
▼ ⚣ ⚢

Williams Lake, B.C. (604)

SERVICES

Cariboo Group
Box 2532, V2G 4P2
PHONE: 392-7343

Province of Manitoba

Manitoba, the province located almost in the dead centre of the country, is a province steeped in turbulent history. It was the home of the Métis-rebellion leader, Louis Riel, and was the centre of extreme native unrest.

Manitoba is divided geographically into two distinct regions: the Canadian Shield, an area covered by forests and rich mining deposits; and the Lowlands, sometimes referred to as "prairietown."

Weatherwise, Manitoba experiences extremes of hot and cold weather. Winter has seen temperatures as low as –40° Celsius. Summer months receive the greatest amount of rainfall.

The Provincial Sales Tax is 7 percent and the legal drinking age is 18. A child of 15 may drink in restaurants if accompanied by parents.

Brandon, Manitoba (204)

SERVICES

Gays/Lesbians of Western Manitoba
P.O. Box 22039, R7A 6Y9
PHONE: 727-4297

WINNIPEG: *A Brief Description*

Winnipeg, called the "Gateway City to Western Canada," due to its central location between eastern and western Canada, was incorporated as a city in 1873, and, with the building of the transcontinental railway in 1881, experienced an economic and migratory boom.

In 1887, with the creation of the Manitoba Grain Exchange, Winnipeg became the grain-market centre for the prairies.

One of the former major Métis settlements and home of Louis Riel is Saint-Boniface, which makes up part of greater Winnipeg. It is considered to be the largest centre of French culture in Canada ouside of Québec.

VISITING WINNIPEG

For visitor information:

Lesbian Resource Line
PHONE: (204) 284-5208

Winnipeg is very cold throughout its long winters; on average, there are only 116 days a year when the temperature is above zero. Due to this invigorating weather, be sure to visit the downtown underground mall and enclosed walkways.

GETTING AROUND WINNIPEG

Highways, railways, and a local airport service this city. Winnipeg transit, the local bus system, costs $1.35 for a one-way fare. Call (204) 284-7190 for more information on local bus routes.

GAY PLACES OF INTEREST

Gay Pride Week, usually held the week closest to the last Sunday in June, and Pink Triangle Day, celebrated on February 14 in remembrance of the gays and lesbians who lost their lives in the Nazi concentration camps during World War II, are events both organized by the Winnipeg Lesbian/Gay Pride Committee. For more information on these events, contact the Lesbian Resource Line.

ENTERTAINMENT

Winnipeg is a city of culture and cultures. It is the home of the Royal Winnipeg Ballet, the Manitoba Theatre Centre, and the Winnipeg Art Gallery.

In February, you can attend the Festival du Voyageur, or in March, there is the Royal Manitoba Winter Fair. Folklorama, a cultural event, is held in August.

There are many summer resorts that offer boating and swimming on Lake Winnipeg, as well as many provincial parks and forests. The Stone Mosaics near Seven Sister Falls is the sacred spot for the Ojibway Indians.

CRUISING AREAS

Cruising is done in a park called "the hill," where a statue of Louis Riel stands, so you can make history and appreciate it at the same time. Public washrooms are not recommended due to increased police presence.

Winnipeg, Manitoba (204)

ACCOMMODATION/BED & BREAKFAST

Winged Ox Guest House
82 Spence St., R3C 1Y3
PHONE/FAX: 783-7408
RATES: $35 single, $50 double
PAYMENT: cash, cheques
▼ ⚣ ⚢

BARS

Club 200
190 Garry St., R3C 1G6
PHONE: 943-6045, FAX: 942-2755
HOURS: Monday to Saturday 4:00 p.m. – 2:00 a.m.

Giovanni's Room
272 Sherbrooke St., R3C 2B9
PHONE: 786-1236
A "private club" (operated by the Oscar Wilde Memorial Society) and a licensed premises, open to everyone. Mostly gay men.
♿ ▼ ⚣ ⚢

Happenings Club
274 Sherbrooke St., R3C 2B9
PHONE: 774-3576

Heartland
298 Fort St., R3C 1E5
PHONE: 957-0635

HOURS: Monday to Thursday 4:00 p.m. – midnight
Friday 4:00 p.m. – 2:00 a.m.
Saturday and Sunday noon – 2:00 a.m.

Ms Purdy's Women's Club
226 Main St., R3C 1A8
PHONE: 989-2344
Remodelled in 1993. Dancing nightly (D.J.), games room, and pool table. Intimate atmosphere. Friendly staff and clientele. On Friday nights, gay men are welcome.
♿ ▼ ⚢

BATHS/SAUNAS

The Office Sauna Bath Ltd.
1060 Main St., R2W 3R7
PHONE: 589-6133
HOURS: Daily 24 hours
PAYMENT: cash, traveller's cheques
▼ ⚣

BOOKSHOPS/LIBRARIES

Dominion News
263 Portage Ave., R3B 2A8
PHONE: 942-6563, FAX: 942-4646

McNally Robinson Booksellers
100 Osborne St., R3L 1Y5
PHONE: 453-2644, FAX: 452-4160
Toll-free: 1-800-561-1833 (Grant Ave. location)
The Osborne Street location of McNally Robinson Booksellers is an arty, urbane little shop with a classy, but comfortable, milieu. Although a general trade bookstore, it has served the gay and lesbian community of Winnipeg well for many years, providing an interesting mix of both gay and lesbian fiction and non-fiction titles. Mail orders accepted.
HOURS: Monday to Friday 9:30 a.m. – 9:30 p.m.
Saturday 9:30 a.m. – 6:00 p.m., Sunday noon – 5:00 p.m.
PAYMENT: cash, personal and traveller's cheques, American Express, MasterCard, VISA
▽ ⚥

CHURCHES/RELIGIOUS ORGANIZATIONS

Dignity/Dignité
P.O. Box 1912, R3C 3R2
PHONE: 786-8633 (Joseph Hunt)
A Roman Catholic support group that meets the third Thursday of each month at 7:30 p.m.
⚣ ⚢

Lutherans Concerned
1 – 120 Donald St.
Box 22034, R3C 4K6
⚣ ⚢

Metropolitan Community Church of Winnipeg
Box 26091, Westminster P.O.
116 Sherbrooke St., R3G 4K9
PHONE: 661-2219
Meets Sundays at 7:30 p.m. at St. Stephen's United Church.
⚣ ⚢

United Church/Affirm
PHONE: 452-2853 (Dave)

PUBLICATIONS

Swerve
Box 31034, 208 – 393 Portage Ave., R3B 3K9
PHONE: 478-1265
Winnipeg's lesbian and gay newspaper. *Swerve* is committed to presenting issues, news, profiles, organization, and calendar listings that are of specific interest to lesbians and gay men in Winnipeg.
PAYMENT: cash, cheques
▼ ⚣ ⚢

RESTAURANTS/CAFÉS

Blue Note Café
220 Main St., R3C 1A8
PHONE: 942-1561

Times Change Café
234 Main St., R3C 1A8
PHONE: 957-0982

The Underground Café
70 Arthur St., R3B 1G7
PHONE: 956-1925

Winona's Coffee & Ice
761 Westminster Ave., R3G 1A6
PHONE: 775-2588
A cozy, neighbourhood café where every table and chair is a work of art. Drop by and sample homemade soups and unique sandwiches. All of this in a smoke-free environment with an array of games and gay publications for customers to enjoy.
HOURS: Monday to Friday 11:00 a.m. – midnight
Saturday and Sunday 10:00 a.m. – midnight
▼ ⚦

RETAIL

Discreet Boutique
317 Ellice Ave., R3B 1X7
PHONE: 947-1307
HOURS: Monday to Friday 10:00 a.m. – 10:00 p.m.
Saturday 10:00 a.m. – 8:00 p.m.
Sunday noon – 5:00 p.m.

FM Underwear
472 Stradbrook, 2nd floor
Osborne Village, R3L 0J9
PHONE: 475-2689

Gathering of Angels
875 Corydon Ave., R3M 0W7
PHONE: 45-Angel

Unique Boutique & Gifts
561 Portage Ave., R3B 2G2
PHONE: 775-5435

SERVICES

Gay/Lesbian Resource Centre

1 – 222 Osborne Ave. S., R3L 1Z3
Mailing address: P.O. Box 1661, R3C 2Z6
PHONE: 284-5208 or 474-0212, FAX: 478-1160
Manitoba's central gay/lesbian community service organization since 1972. Offers a phone line, library, archives, education and advocacy services. Publishes a monthly called *The Alternative*. Also provides speakers on gay/lesbian rights and homophobia.
HOURS: Monday to Friday 1:00 p.m. – 4:30 p.m. &
7:30 p.m. – 10:00 p.m.
PAYMENT: cash, cheques
▼ ⚣ ⚢

TRAVEL/TOURS

Out 'N About Travel

207 – 100 Osborne St. S.
McKim Courtyard, R3L 1Y5
PHONE: 477-6799, FAX: 475-9493
Toll-free: 1-800-254-5552
HOURS: Monday to Friday 8:30 a.m. – 5:00 p.m.
Saturday 10:00 a.m. – 2:00 p.m.

Province of Ontario

As the song goes, "Good things grow in Ontario," and we have the growing gay and lesbian scene to prove it. Stratford is perhaps Ontario's gay haven for theatre-loving queers. The Ottawa/Hull region's gay and lesbian community is ever increasing, with several gay and lesbian bars and publications. By far the largest and most established gay scene, however, is found in the province's capital city of Toronto.

For those who like it rough, the wilderness of northern Ontario's Algonquin Park offers fabulous opportunities for canoeing and camping (we mean the kind where you use a sleeping bag).

Ontario's Provincial Sales Tax is 8 percent, and the legal drinking age is 19.

Acton, Ontario (519)

SERVICES

PFLAG
PHONE: 853-0382 (Barbara, contact only)

Barrie, Ontario (705)

BARS

Graydons & Co.
147 Dunlop St. E., L4M 1A6
PHONE: 728-3418

SERVICES

AIDS Committee
80 Bradford St., Unit 20B, L4N 3A8
PHONE: 722-6778, FAX: 722-6560

Brampton, Ontario (416)

SERVICES

PFLAG
Contact: Mary Jones
PHONE: 457-4570
No active meetings anymore. Simply a contact.

Cambridge, Ontario (519)

BARS

Otherside
22 Dickson St., N1R 1T4
PHONE: 622-9417

SERVICES

PFLAG
PHONE: 623-0492 (Mary, contact only)

Edwards, Ontario (613)

ACCOMMODATION/BED & BREAKFAST

Stone House B&B
2605 Yorkes Corners Rd.
RR#1, KOA 1GO
PHONE: 821-3822, FAX: 567-0752
[*Editor's note*: A country estate 25 minutes from downtown Ottawa.]

Fort Erie, Ontario (905)

BATHS/SAUNAS

Fort Erie Steam Baths
216 Jarvis St., L2A 2S5
PHONE: 871-0023

Grand Valley, Ontario (519)

ACCOMMODATION/BED & BREAKFAST

Manfred's Meadow Guest House
RR#1, LON 1GO
PHONE: 925-5306
Manfred's Meadow is a relaxing place: a retreat where you can do whatever you like — or nothing at all. The main farmhouse is found in a parklike setting. The log house is over 100 years old. The property has 100 acres to roam. No one has ever left hungry — all meals included.
PAYMENT: cash, personal and traveller's cheques
▼ ⚣ ⚢

Guelph, Ontario (519)

RESTAURANTS/CAFÉS

Bookshelf Café
41 Quebec St., N1H 2T1
PHONE: 821-3311

Street Grill
31 Yarmouth St., N1H 4G2
PHONE: 763-6460

SERVICES

Gayline Guelph
PHONE: 836-4550
Puts out a newsletter and operates a phone line.
HOURS: Monday and Wednesday for women 7:30 p.m. – 9:30 p.m.
Tuesday and Thursday for men 7:30 p.m. – 9:30 p.m.

SERVICES

PFLAG
PHONE: 822-6912 (Grace or Bill)
Meetings: Third Friday of each month

Hamilton, Ontario (905)

ACCOMMODATION/BED & BREAKFAST

Windsor Hotel Hamilton Limited
31 John St. N., L8R 1H2
PHONE: 522-5990
A happy, relaxing atmosphere where gays and lesbians feel at home. Canadian cuisine, pizza, and panzerotti served.
♿ ▽ ⚣ ⚢

BARS

Café 121/Club 121
121 Hughson St. N., L8R 1G7
PHONE: 546-5258
Large converted warehouse with casual, inexpensive dining room on the first level; neighbourhood pub atmosphere in Amigo's Back Bar. There is a second-floor hi-tech dance bar and basement leather bar.
▼ ⚣ ⚢

Embassy Club
54 King St. E., L8N 1A6
PHONE: 522-7783

X-Club
31 John St. N., L8R 1H2
PHONE: 526-1946

BOOKSHOPS/LIBRARIES

Women's Bookstop
333 Main St. W., L8P 1K1
PHONE: 525-2970

RESTAURANTS/CAFÉS

Café 121/Club 121
(See entry under BARS heading.)

SERVICES

AIDS Network
143 James St. S., Suite 900, L8P 3A1
PHONE: 528-0854, FAX: 528-6311
HOURS: Monday to Thursday 9:00 a.m. – 9:00 p.m.
Friday 9:00 a.m. – 5:00 p.m.

Huntsville, Ontario (416)

ACCOMMODATION/BED & BREAKFAST

Eagle's Nest
Osborne Pt. Rd.
RR#2, POA 1KO
PHONE: 967-3896
[*Editor's note*: For PWAS, HIV+, and caregiver's only.]

Jasper, Ontario (613)

ACCOMMODATION/BED & BREAKFAST

Starr Easton Hall
P.O. Box 215, RR#3, KOG 1GO
PHONE: 283-7497
Located at the corner of Kilmarnock Rd. and County Rd. #16. This country inn and restaurant is a restored Victorian country home set in a 10-acre garden. It is located midway between Ottawa and the St. Lawrence Seaway near the Rideau Canal. Starr Easton Hall is the perfect setting for receptions, private parties, and quiet getaways. Reservations are recommended. The Inn has a fully licensed dining room and a gift shop.
PAYMENT: cash, personal and traveller's cheques, MasterCard, VISA
♿ ▼ ⚢

Kingston, Ontario (613)

BARS

Robert's Club Vogue
477 Princess St., K7L 1C3
PHONE: 547-2923

A night club with a dance floor, playing the latest in dance music. Three pool tables, video games, a restaurant, and three bars — one of them a country and western bar. The only gay bar between Toronto and Ottawa. Washrooms are not wheelchair accessible.
HOURS: Daily 4:00 p.m. – 3:00 a.m.
PAYMENT: cash, MasterCard, VISA
▼ ⚧

RESTAURANTS/CAFÉS

Chinese Laundry Café
291 Princess St., K7L 1B4
PHONE: 542-2282
The café, located in downtown Kingston, serves a menu of soups, salads, sandwiches, and patés with lots of vegetarian options, but is still best known for its ever-changing selection of over 20 desserts, baked fresh daily.
PAYMENT: cash, INTERAC, MasterCard, VISA
♿ ▽ ⚧ ♀

SERVICES

AIDS Committee
848A Princess St., K7L 1G7
PHONE: 545-3698
HOURS: Monday to Friday 9:00 a.m. – 4:30 p.m.

Kingston Lesbian, Gay, Bisexual Association
51 Queen's Cres., K7L 2S7
PHONE: 545-2960
The LGBA has a phone line staffed by trained volunteers, Monday to Friday nights, a lending library of fiction, non-fiction, and current lesbian and gay newspapers, and a speaker's bureau which will address groups and classes.
HOURS: Monday to Friday 7:00 p.m. – 9:00 p.m.

PFLAG
PHONE: 546-0267

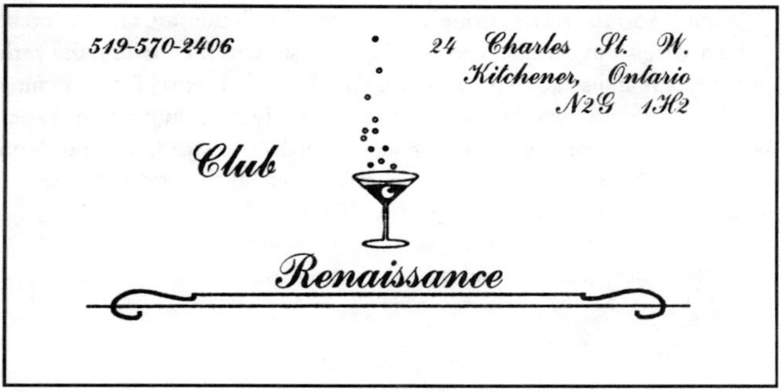

Kitchener, Ontario (519)

BARS

Club Renaissance
24 Charles St. W., N2G 1H2
PHONE: 570-2406
Featuring fresh D.J.'s who spin hot wax! Friendly staff and atmosphere. An evening of affordable entertainment.
HOURS: Wednesday to Sunday 9:00 p.m. – 2:00 a.m.
Thursday and Friday 9:00 p.m. – 3:00 a.m.
PAYMENT: cash, traveller's cheques
▼ ⚣ ⚢

Lakefield, Ontario (705)

ACCOMMODATION/BED & BREAKFAST

Windmere Farm Bed & Breakfast
Selwyn, RR#3, K0L 2H0
PHONE: 652-6290, FAX: 652-6949
Toll-free: 1-800-465-6327

Windmere Farm is an 1845 stone home, restored with care, art, and Victorian antiques. Relax in the very private efficiency suite or the studio room with private bath and sauna. Enjoy the walking trails and spring-fed swimming pond. Air-conditioned. No pets or smoking. Only ten minutes from Peterborough. Directions (from Peterborough): north on Hwy 28, then north on Hwy 507 to Selwyn. Turn right at Selwyn and left at the first farm gate.
RATES: $35 single, $45 to $55 double, $65 suite, $10 extra person
HOURS: Daily 8:00 a.m. – 8:00 p.m.
PAYMENT: cash, personal and traveller's cheques
▽ ⚢

London, Ontario (519)

BARS

52nd Street
347 Clarence St., N6H 3M4
PHONE: 679-4015
[*Editor's note*: Mixed dance bar. Gay-friendly.]

HALO Inc.
649 Colborne St., N6A 3Z2
PHONE: 433-3762
Gayline: 433-3551
A lesbian and gay community centre with a licensed bar, a coffeehouse, and women's dances, as well as a gayline. HALO is also the name of their publication. Wheelchair accessible only on licensed floor. Also listed under SERVICES heading.
HOURS: *Bar*: Wednesday 9:00 p.m. – midnight
Friday and Saturday 9:00 p.m. – 1:00 a.m.
Women's dances: held last Thursday of each month
Coffee House: Monday 7:00 p.m. – 10:00 p.m.
Gayline: Monday and Thursday 7:00 p.m. – 10:00 p.m.
PAYMENT: cash, VISA
▼ ⚣ ⚢

Lacy's
355 Talbot St., N6A 2R5
PHONE: 645-3197

BATHS/SAUNAS

Club London
722 York St. (rear), N5W 2S6
PHONE: 438-2625
Club London is the only gay bath/spa/health club in London. It also provides information about London and surrounding area gay bars, baths, and organizations.
RATES: $15 room for eight hours
$7 locker for eight hours
HOURS: Daily 24 hours
PAYMENT: cash only
▼ ⚣

BOOKSHOPS/LIBRARIES

Womansline Books
711 Richmond St., N6A 3H1
PHONE: 679-3416
A feminist bookstore including a complete collection of lesbian and gay fiction and non-fiction as well as women's music, jewellery, etc. Catalogues available and mail orders accepted.
HOURS: Monday to Thursday 10:00 a.m. – 5:30 p.m.
Friday 10:00 a.m. – 6:00 p.m.
Saturday 10:00 a.m. – 5:30 p.m.
PAYMENT: cash, personal and traveller's cheques, MasterCard, VISA
▼ ⚣ ⚢ ♀

CHURCHES/RELIGIOUS ORGANIZATIONS

Dignity London Dignité
P.O. Box 1884, Station A, N6A 5J4
PHONE: 686-7709 after 5:00 p.m.
For homosexual and lesbian Catholics and their friends. Information night is the second Monday of each month from 7:30 p.m. – 8:30 p.m.
⚣ ⚢

Metropolitan Community Church of London
P.O. Box 213, Station B, N6A 4B8
PHONE: 645-0744
Sundays at 7:20 p.m. at corner of William Street and Queens Avenue.
⚣ ⚢

PUBLICATIONS

London Pink Pathways
P.O. Box 33009, 1299 Oxford St. E., N5Y 1A0
PHONE: 473-0495, FAX: 471-6013

RESTAURANTS/CAFÉS

Blackfriars Café
46 Blackfriars St., N6H 1K7
PHONE: 667-4930

Green Tomatoes
172 King St., N6A 1C6
PHONE: 660-1170

Verandah Café
546 Dundas St., N6B 1W8
PHONE: 434-6790
A small, intimate dining room with a mature clientele and a continental menu. Four-star rated. Reservations are required, but the dress code is casual. Licensed to sell beer and alcohol.
HOURS: Tuesday to Friday 11:30 a.m. – 2:00 p.m.
Tuesday to Saturday 5:30 p.m. – 9:00 p.m.
▼ ⚤

SERVICES

AIDS Committee of London
Suite 200 – 343 Richmond St., N6A 2C3
PHONE: 434-1601, FAX: 434-1843

HIV/AIDS service organization providing extensive support to people living with HIV and people affected by HIV/AIDS in any way. Comprehensive resource centre, speakers, safer sex presentations, condoms, brochures, and education services. Wheelchair accessible with assistance.
HOURS: Monday to Thursday 9:00 a.m. – 9:00 p.m.
Friday 9:00 a.m. – 5:00 p.m.
♿ ▽ ⚥

Homophile Association of London Ontario (HALO Inc.)
649 Colborne St., N6A 3Z2
PHONE: 433-3762
Gayline: 433-3551 (Monday, Wednesday, Thursday 7:00 p.m. – 10:00 p.m.)
(See HALO under BARS heading.)

OTHER

SWON
PHONE: 434-7018
Male-only group of southwestern Ontario nudists that meets once per month. Call for more info.

Maynooth, Ontario (613)

ACCOMMODATION/BED & BREAKFAST

Wildewood Guest House
Madawaska Rd., Box 121, K0L 2S0
PHONE/FAX: 338-3134
Located 30 minutes from Algonquin Park, Wildewood Guest House offers peace and quiet "far from the madding crowd." Two rooms with views, three meals a day, and no taxes.
RATES: $125 weekdays
$137.50 weekends
HOURS: Daily 9:00 a.m. – 9:00 p.m. for inquiries by phone.
PAYMENT: cash, personal and traveller's cheques
♿ ▼ ⚣ ⚢

Mississauga, Ontario (905)

BARS

Go West
105 Lakeshore Rd. E., L2G 1E2
PHONE: 891-6911
⚣ ⚢

RETAIL

Fun Fashions
1129 Derry Rd. E., L5T 1P3
PHONE: 670-9551

Oshawa, Ontario (905)

BARS

The Bar
110 Dundas St. W.
Whitby, Ontario L1N 2L9
HOURS: Daily 7:00 p.m. – 4:00 a.m.
[*Editor's note*: Durham region's only gay bar.]

CHURCHES/RELIGIOUS ORGANIZATIONS

Seventh-Day Adventist Kinship Canada
P.O. Box 82578, 5 Points Mall Postal Outlet, L1G 7W7
PHONE: 432-2867
Spiritual, emotional, and social support to present or former SDAs who are gay or lesbian.

SERVICES

Durham Alliance Association
PHONE: 434-4297
HOURS: Saturday 8:00 p.m. – 1:00 a.m.

OTTAWA: *A Brief Description*

Ottawa is Canada's capital city and home to the federal parliament offices and legislative buildings. Because it is located so close to the Québec border, you will find French being spoken here, especially across the river in Hull. Hull is actually Ottawa's twin city on the Québec side, but it is usually included with Ottawa. Hull, being part of Québec, shares Québec's drinking age of 18. Ottawa, however, is part of Ontario, and the drinking age is 19.

VISITING OTTAWA

For visitor information:

Ottawa Tourism & Conv. Authority at National Arts Centre

or

Association Touristique de l'Outaouais
25 Laurier
Hull, Québec J8X 4C8
PHONE: (819) 778-2222

For information on gay places of interest:
PHONE: (613) 238-1717

Ottawa has hot, humid summers and cold winters. Downtown Ottawa is divided into east and west by the Rideau Canal.

GETTING AROUND

Flights to Ottawa land at the Ottawa International Airport. Bus routes include the Ottawa transit system and the Outaouais transit system in Hull. Bus fares are $1.30 during regular hours, and $2.00 in peak hours (6 – 9:30 a.m. and 3 – 5:30 p.m.). Ottawa also has an extensive system of bicycle paths lined with bright flowers in spring, to make getting around more enjoyable.

GAY PLACES OF INTEREST

Ottawa's gay community is located in an area called "Centretown," and the area's gay bars and baths lie a few blocks west of Elgin Street.

Gay Pride Day is officially recognized here, and is celebrated one week before Toronto's (usually on the second-last Sunday in June). Call the local gayline for more information.

ENTERTAINMENT

During the cold winter months, the Rideau Canal is transformed into the world's largest skating rink. February marks the 10-day Winterlude — a winter carnival with spectacular ice sculptures and outdoor sporting activities (you can take care of the indoor ones).

In May there is the popular week-long Festival of Spring where outdoor beer gardens, flea markets, and fireworks are everywhere. Go and see the sparks fly!

The July 1 Canada Day celebrations in the nation's capital offer a fabulous fireworks display, and turn the usually quiet Ottawa into Partytown.

CRUISING AREAS

The largest and relatively safest cruising area is Remic Rapids Park. It is approximately a five-minute drive from downtown Ottawa, and the action is jumping day or night. Other cruising areas include Rockcliff park, which is most active during the day; the Rideau Canal is an unofficial nighttime cruising spot, but we've been informed that this area is known to bashers, so be careful.

Be aware: each of the following cruising spots has been labelled a "high risk" area by the Ottawa Bias Crime Unit, with each experiencing a marked rise in gay bashings. McKenzie Street (predominantly a gay hustling area),

Major Hill Park, and the Rideau Shopping Centre (most active during the winter months, in washrooms). If you cruise these locations, exercise caution.

Ottawa, Ontario (613)

ACCOMMODATION/BED & BREAKFAST

Rideau View Inn
177 Frank St., K2P 0X4
PHONE: 236-9309, FAX: 237-6842
Toll-free: 1-800-268-2082
Rideau View Inn is a 1907 home located in the centre of Ottawa, within walking distance of Parliament Hill, fine dining, and shopping. Tennis courts and the Rideau Canal are a few steps away.
RATES: $65 to $75
HOURS: Daily 8:00 a.m. – 10:30 p.m.
PAYMENT: cash, traveller's cheques, American Express, MasterCard, VISA
▼ ⚢

BARS

Bar 318
318 Lisgar St., K2P 5W9
c/o ALGBO (see AGLBO under SERVICES listing)
[*Editor's note*: Saturday nights are for women.]

Calvin's Exotic Dance Club
151 George St., 3rd floor, K1N 5W5
PHONE: 241-7017

Centretown Pub/Cell Block/Silhouette Piano Bar
340 Somerset St. W., K2P 0J9
PHONE: 594-0233
⚣ ⚢

The Club/Clubhouse
77 Wellington St., Hull J8X 2H7
PHONE: (819) 777-1411
[*Editor's note*: The Club is mixed and the Clubhouse upstairs is for women.]

Club 363
363 Bank St., K2P 1X9
PHONE: 237-0708
⚣

Coral Reef
30 Nicholas St., K1N 7B8
(entrance to parking garage)
PHONE: 234-5118
[*Editor's note*: Friday nights for women only.]
⚣ ⚢

Detour Bar
283 Dalhousie St., K1N 7E5
PHONE: 241-4646, FAX: 727-5070
Party with Detour Bar, Ottawa's newest dance bar. Mostly men aged 19 – 50. Draft on tap. Rooftop patio. Downstairs men's bar. Entertainment on Thursdays and Sundays are for tea (4:00 p.m. – 7:00 p.m.) or line dancing (7:00 p.m. – 10:00 p.m.).

HOURS: Daily 9:00 a.m. – 2:00 p.m.
PAYMENT: cash, traveller's cheques, American Express, MasterCard, VISA
♿ ▼ ⚣ ⚢

Market Station
15 George St., K1N 8W5
PHONE: 562-3540

Pub de la Promenade
175 du Portage, Hull, J8X 2K4
PHONE: (819) 771-8810
⚥

BATHS/SAUNAS

Club Ottawa
1069 Wellington St., K1Y 2Y2
PHONE: 722-8978
Located near the downtown area, Ottawa's only licensed bathhouse has single and double rooms, TV lounge, universal gym, tanning room, sauna, in and out privileges extended to 24-hour customers, beer, wine, and liquor.
HOURS: Daily 24 hours.
PAYMENT: cash, INTERAC, VISA
▼ ⚣

Steamworks
487 Lewis St., K2P 0T2
PHONE: 230-8431, FAX: 231-4260
Ottawa's newest sauna for men located in the downtown core, close to the clubs.
HOURS: Daily 24 hours
PAYMENT: cash, American Express, MasterCard, VISA
▼ ⚣

BOOKSHOPS/LIBRARIES

After Stonewall
105 – 4th Ave., 2nd floor, K1S 2L1
PHONE: 567-2221, FAX: 567-0752
While primarily a bookstore offering the best and latest in gay/lesbian fiction and non-fiction, After Stonewall also carries mags, cards, art books, t-shirts,

lubricants, and a wide range of quality gift items. Mail orders are accepted.
HOURS: Monday to Thursday, Saturday 10:00 a.m. – 6:00 p.m.
Friday 10:00 a.m. – 7:30 p.m., Sunday noon – 4:00 p.m.
PAYMENT: cash, personal and traveller's cheques, MasterCard, VISA
▼ ⚣ ⚢

Mother Tongue Books
1067 Bank St., K1S 3W9
PHONE: 730-2346

Ottawa Women's Bookstore
272 Elgin St., K2P 1M2
PHONE: 230-1156
More than a bookstore — provides listings of community events, housing file, ticket outlet, and general community gathering place.
Mail orders accepted.
HOURS: Monday to Wednesday 10:00 a.m. – 6:00 p.m.
Thursday and Friday 10:00 a.m. – 9:00 p.m.
Saturday 10:00 a.m. – 6:00 p.m.
PAYMENT: cash, personal and traveller's cheques, MasterCard, VISA
♿ ▼ ⚢

Pink Triangle Services Library
318 Lisgar St., K2P 5W9 c/o ALGBO
(See ALGBO under SERVICES heading.)
PHONE: 563-4818

CHURCHES/RELIGIOUS ORGANIZATIONS

Dignity Ottawa Dignité
P.O. Box 2102, Station D, K1P 5W3
PHONE: 746-7279, FAX: 746-0353
⚣ ⚢

Metropolitan Community Church of Ottawa/ Église Communautaire Metropolitaine d'Ottawa
P.O. Box 41082, 1910 St. Laurent Blvd, K1G 5K9
PHONE: 232-0241
Worships on Sundays at 4:00 p.m. at Pink Triangle Services on 71 Bank Street (2nd floor). Also meets at 7:30 p.m. on Tuesdays at a member's home. Gay, lesbian, bisexual positive Christian.
♿ ▼ ⚢

PUBLICATIONS

Capital Xtra!

303 – 177 Nepean St., K2P 0B4
PHONE: 237-7133, FAX: 237-6651
Other Numbers: Tel-A-Guide 237-XTRA (24-hour touch-tone guide to Ottawa/Hull gay and lesbian community)
XTC (*Capital Xtra*'s Talking Classifieds) 237-5554 (24-hour telephone dating for lesbians and gay men)
Cruiseline 237-5554 (all-male live phone connections — 24 hour)
Capital Xtra is Ottawa's only professional monthly newspaper devoted to gay and lesbian news and entertainment. Thirteen thousand copies monthly.
HOURS: Monday to Friday 9:00 a.m. – 6:00 p.m.
PAYMENT: cash, personal cheques, MasterCard, VISA
▼ ⚣ ⚢

Go Info

P.O. Box 2919, Station D, K1P 5W9
PHONE: 238-8990, FAX: 748-0076
Go Info is a bilingual newspaper published primarily by and for gays, lesbians, and bisexuals in the national-capital region. It provides information relevant to lesbians, gays, and bisexuals and is a forum for debate and creative expression.
▼ ⚣ ⚢

Labrys
Box 81104, K1P 1A5
PHONE/FAX: 237-6150
This bimonthly wants to raise the profile of lesbians by providing a lesbian perspective on the events in our lives and by promoting events lesbians will enjoy.
PAYMENT: cash, personal cheques
▼ ⚢

Malebox Magazine
P.O. Box 166, Station B, K1P 5P6
PHONE/FAX: 234-2191
Canada's only national all-male classifieds. Hot stories, photos — the irreverent sex mag that has all Canada talking.
PAYMENT: cash, personal and traveller's cheques, money orders
▼ ⚣

The Womanist
41 York St., 3rd floor, K1N 5S7
PHONE: 562-4081, FAX: 562-4033
The Womanist is a national feminist newspaper distributed in 75 communities in Canada.
♿ ▼ ♀

RESTAURANTS/CAFÉS

Blue Moon
311 Bank St., K2P 1X9
PHONE: 230-1239

Manfred's Restaurant
2280 Carling Ave., K2B 7G1
PHONE: 829-5715
Serving international cuisine, specializing in fine European dishes.
♿ ▽ ⚥

The News
284 Elgin St., K2P 1M3
PHONE: 567-6397
▼

The Tea Party
103 4th Ave., K1S 2L1
PHONE: 238-5031

William Street Café
47 William St., K1N 6Z9
PHONE: 241-4254

RETAIL

Mags & Fags
286 Elgin, K2P 1M3
PHONE: 233-9651

Marc's Smoke Shop
420 Rideau St., K1N 5Z1
PHONE: 789-8886
[*Editor's note*: Gay videos, adult toys, and condoms.]

Papery
11A William St., K1N 9C7
PHONE: 241-1212

Video 2000 Plus
691 St. Joseph Blvd., Hull, J8Y 4B4
PHONE: (819) 777-3527

Wilde's
631 Somerset St. W., K1R 5K3
PHONE: 567-4858
▼ ⚣ ⚢

SERVICES

AIDS Committee of Ottawa
207 Queen St., 4th floor, K1P 6E5
PHONE: 238-5014, FAX: 238-3425
The AIDS Committee of Ottawa is a volunteer-based community service organization. ACO formed in 1985 to meet the needs of people affected by AIDS. Services include support services, public education, advocacy, and personal development.
♿ ▽ ⚥

Association of Lesbians, Gays, & Bisexuals of Ottawa (ALGBO)

318 Lisgar St., K2P 5W9

PHONE: 233-0152, FAX: 748-0076

ALGBO is a community association which operates a community centre, Friday night coffeehouse, Saturday night women's bar, a newspaper (*Go Info*), and a political action committee.

HOURS: Monday to Friday 7:30 p.m. – 10:00 p.m.

▼ ⚣ ⚢

Canadian AIDS Society — National AIDS Coalition

400 – 100 Sparks St., K1P 5B7

PHONE: 230-3580, FAX: 563-4998

A national coalition of more than 100 community-based AIDS organizations providing services to member groups as well as lobbying the federal government on various HIV/AIDS issues.

HOURS: Monday to Friday 8:30 a.m. – 5:30 p.m.

♿ ▽ ⚥

Gayline

PHONE: 238-1717

HOURS: Daily 7:00 p.m. – 10:00 p.m.

Lambda Ottawa

P.O. Box 1445, Station B, K1P 5P6

PHONE: 233-8212 for recorded message

Ottawa's lesbian and gay social group addressing the interests of business, professionals, arts, and entertainment and their friends and families.

TRAVEL/TOURS

Far Horizons Inc.

190 Maclaren St., K2P 0L6

PHONE: 234-6116, FAX: 563-2593

Full-service, gay-positive travel agency. Guaranteed lowest rates.

▽ ⚥

GetAway Travel

380 Elgin St., K2P 1N1

PHONE: 230-2250, FAX: 230-3396

Toll-free: 1-800-699-6193

GetAway Travel is a full-service travel agency as well as tour operator offering packages from the United States to Canada. Packages as low as $450 U.S. for one week on FIT or group basis.

HOURS: Monday to Wednesday 10:00 a.m. – 6:00 p.m.
Thursday to Friday 10:00 a.m. – 9:00 p.m.
Saturday 11:00 a.m. – 5:00 p.m.

PAYMENT: cash, personal and traveller's cheques, MasterCard, VISA

▼ ⚥

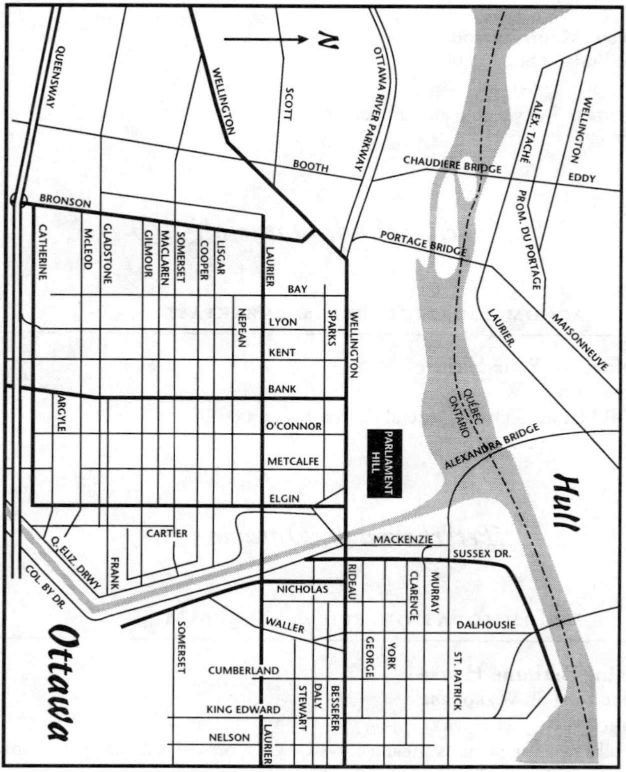

Ottawa City Hall Tours
PHONE: 564-1400 one day in advance
HOURS: Monday to Friday 9:00 a.m. – 3:00 p.m.
Guided tours are 45 minutes each and there is free parking.

OTHER

Defiant Voices
CKCU 93.1 FM
HOURS: Wednesday at 6:00 p.m.
⚣ ⚢

New Moon Tattoo
80 Burland St., K2B 6K1
PHONE: 596-1790
HOURS: Daily 2:00 p.m. – 10:00 p.m.
▽ ⚧

Owen Sound, Ontario (519)

ACCOMMODATION/BED & BREAKFAST

Nurture Your Nature
508 13th St. W.
OR Mailing address: General Delivery, N4K 3X1
PHONE: 372-2854

Peterborough, Ontario (705)

ACCOMMODATION/BED & BREAKFAST

King Bethune House
270 King St. W., K9J 2S2
PHONE: 743-4101, FAX: 745-9775
Full breakfast menu is included. AAA/CAA approved. Clientele is mainly business, arts, and professional people.

RATES: $50/$60 double (one/two people)
$70/$80 Queen Bethune room
$100/$110 King Bethune room
PAYMENT: cash, cheques, American Express, MasterCard, VISA
▽ ⚧

Port Sydney, Ontario (705)

ACCOMMODATION/BED & BREAKFAST

Divine Lake Resort
RR#1, Box XD3, POB 1L0
PHONE: 385-1212, FAX: 385-1283
Toll-free: 1-800-263-6600
Primarily a hotel/resort with a bar and health club. Probably the largest gay resort in Canada, with chalets and cottages for up to 60 guests. Nestled at beautiful Divine Lake on 86 acres of total privacy. Food served is Canadian/European and vegetarian. Reservations are required. Partially wheelchair accessible.
RATES: $89 – $128 per person per night including meals.
▼ ⚣ ⚢

Simcoe County, Ontario (705)

SERVICES

AIDS Committee of Simcoe County
PHONE: 722-6778, FAX: 722-6560

Gay and Lesbian Association of Simcoe County (GLASC)
P.O. Box 2224, Orillia, Ontario, L3Z 6S1
PHONE: 325-0033
Sometimes phone line is staffed and other times there is an answering machine. This organization puts out a newsletter called *The Umbrella*.

St. Catharines, Ontario (905)

SERVICES

AIDS Committee
50 William St., Suite 200, L2R 5J2
PHONE: 984-8684
HOURS: Monday to Friday 8:30 a.m. – 4:30 p.m.

STRATFORD: *A Brief Description*

Stratford is named after Stratford-Upon-Avon in England, and, like its sister city, Stratford, Ontario, has a river running through it called the Avon. Stratford is home to the famous Festival Theatre and Shakespearean Garden, where Shakespeare fans flock every summer.

The town of Stratford is divided into five wards: Romeo, Hamlet, Falstaff, Avon, and Shakespeare. Here's a juicy tidbit for all you lesbians: Stratford's civic flower is the IRIS!

Watch for the swans who like to stroll around downtown.

VISITING STRATFORD

For visitor information:

Tourism Stratford
88 Wellington St., Stratford, Ontario N5A 2L2
PHONE: 1-800-561-SWAN, 271-5140 (in Stratford), 273-3352

In the summer months, the days are hot, followed by cool nights. Stratford winters start in early November, with cold and snow lasting until the end of March.

Keep in mind, even with the presence of an established theatre community, there is not an active "out" gay and lesbian community in Stratford.

GETTING AROUND STRATFORD

Stratford has a local bus route, and a one-trip fare costs under one dollar. Walking around the town is very enjoyable, due to the beautiful scenery and the river. Stratford municipal airport has added a new terminal building and has modern facilities. For a tour of Stratford, you can take a ride on a double-decker bus that offers tours three times a day. For more information, contact Tourism Stratford.

GAY PLACES OF INTEREST

There are two bars in Stratford that are considered to be local gay hangouts, although neither is specifically gay. The first is Bentley's, Stratford's local bar and inn, where a large queer presence is found. The other is called Down the Street — so named because it is located just down the street from the popular Bentley's.

ENTERTAINMENT

Stratford is primarily a summer theatre town, with shows usually running from May to October. Three theatres in Stratford — the Avon Theatre, the Festival Theatre, and the Tom Patterson Theatre — host an annually changing repertoire of Shakesperean plays, musicals, and other historical and modern productions.

To contact the Stratford Festival box office, call 1-519-273-1600, or toll-free at 1-800-567-1600 for reservations and tickets.

CRUISING AREAS

The cruising areas in Stratford are mainly restricted to the bars and the river after dark.

Stratford, Ontario (519)

ACCOMMODATION/BED & BREAKFAST

Anything Goes Bed & Breakfast

107 Huron St., N5A 5S7
PHONE: 273-6557
Cole Porter would feel right at home! Edwardian elegance with a relaxed, "anything goes" atmosphere. Creative breakfasts, separate parlour for guests, smoking on the verandah. Reservations are required.
RATES: $55 double or twin and shared bath
$80 queen-size bed with ensuite bath
HOURS: Daily 8:00 a.m. – midnight
▼ ⚤

Bentley's Inn & Restaurant

99 Ontario St., N5A 3H1
PHONE: 271-1121, FAX: 272-1853
⚣ ⚢ ⚤

Burnside Guest Home

139 William St., N5A 4X9
PHONE: 271-7076
Burnside is an ancestral turn-of-the-century home which is situated on the north shore of Lake Victoria. Special weekend packages can be arranged during the off season. Write or phone for information. We serve a full home-cooked breakfast which will delight any appetite.
RATES: $25 for students
$55 double or twin with shared bath
$65 for king-size bed
HOURS: Daily 7:00 a.m. – 11:30 p.m.
PAYMENT: cash, US cash, personal and traveller's cheques, MasterCard
▼ ⚤

The Maples of Stratford B&B

220 Church St., N5A 2R6
PHONE: 273-0810

BARS

Bentley's Inn & Restaurant
(See under ACCOMMODATION/BED & BREAKFAST heading)

Down the Street
30 Ontario St., N5A 3G8
PHONE: 273-5886

Jay's Bar & Grill
23 Albert St., N5A 3K2
PHONE: 271-1023, FAX: 271-8487

Old English Parlour
101 Wellington St., N5A 2L4
PHONE: 271-2772

BOOKSHOPS/LIBRARIES

Book Vault
131 Ontario St., N5A 3H1
PHONE: 271-6310

Fanfare Books
92 Ontario St., N5A 3H2
PHONE: 273-1010

GALLERIES

Gerard Brender à Brandis
Bookwright and Wood Engraver
249 Ontario St., N5A 3H6
PHONE: 273-7523
The studio of a working artist/craftsperson providing original prints, drawings, paintings, and handmade books. Papermaking, illustration, printing, bookbinding, spinning and weaving as well as oil painting, watercolours, and scratch board. Located in central Stratford within walking distance of the three theatres. Open May 15 to November 15.
HOURS: Wednesday to Sunday 10:00 a.m. – 6:00 p.m.
PAYMENT: cash, personal and traveller's cheques, VISA
▼ ⚢

RESTAURANTS/CAFÉS

Boar's Head (at Queen's Inn)
161 Ontario St., N5A 3H3
PHONE: 271-1400

Cece's Tea and Coffee House
72 Wellington St., N5A 2L2
PHONE: 272-0917

Old Prune
151 Albert St., N5A 3K5
PHONE: 271-5052

Sudbury, Ontario (705)

BARS

D Bar
83 Cedar St., P3E 1A7
PHONE: 670-1189
High-energy dance club. Theme nights all week, dance room, lounge, and billiards room. Open to all ages.
HOURS: Daily 5:00 p.m. – 1:00 a.m. (until 3:00 a.m. on weekends)
♿ ▼ ⚣ ⚢

TRAVEL/TOURS

Wild Women Expeditions
P.O. Box 145, Station B, P3E 4N5
PHONE: 866-1260
Wild Women Expeditions offers women fun outdoor and canoeing adventures in northern Ontario. Enjoy the beauty and challenge of paddling through spectacular lakes and rivers. All equipment and food supplied, plus a friendly, experienced guide. Arts programs and spirituality weekends are also held at our base camp. Over 200 acres with cabins, swimming, and sauna. See travel section at the end of the guide for specific details.
▼ ⚢ ♀

Thunder Bay, Ontario (807)

BOOKSHOPS/LIBRARIES

Northern Women's Bookstore
65 South Court St., P7B 2X2
PHONE: 344-7979
HOURS: Tuesday to Saturday 11:00 a.m. – 6:00 p.m.

PUBLICATIONS

Northern Women's Journal
P.O. Box 144, P7C 4V5

TORONTO: *A Brief Description*

For sheer diversity, Toronto has no rivals. There are many sub-regions to this city, including Little Italy, Chinatown, Indiatown, Greektown, and our favourite, the Gay Ghetto, located at the corner of Church and Wellesley Streets.

VISITING TORONTO

For visitor information:

Metro Toronto CVA
207 Queen's Quay W., Suite 509
Toronto, Ontario M5J 1A7
PHONE: 1-800-363-1990

For information on gay events:
PHONE: 964-6600
Summers in Toronto are generally hot and humid from June to August, with cooler weather in the fall months. Winters are cold, with the odd blizzard

that can shut down businesses for a day. Spring starts in early to mid-April, and is fairly rainy and breezy.

GETTING AROUND TORONTO

The Toronto airport is called the Lester B. Pearson International Airport, and it is located just west of the city. There are buses to get to the centre of Toronto, and taxi services are also available.

The TTC, Toronto's transit system, includes a subway system similar to New York's (some would consider Toronto's cleaner), with streetcars, bus routes, and an LRT route.

Adult fares are $2.00 (exact change) for a one-way trip, or ten tickets for $13.00. Adults may purchase a "two-fare" ticket for $3.00, or buy a day pass allowing a day's worth of unlimited transit use for $5.00. Children under the age of two ride free. Children under the age of twelve ride for $0.50 one way or eight tickets for $2.50.

Many of the streetcars operate 24 hours, but the subway does close down at 2:00 a.m. Call 393-INFO for general information about bus schedules, costs, and directions. Cabs are easy to flag downtown. There are many car rental outlets, but there is little parking and what is available is costly. Downtown Toronto, in the summer months, also has rickshaws pulled by students. They should cost around $1.00 per block — if you are charged $5.00 per block, then you are being ripped off.

Toronto also has several bike trails. Also offered are walking tours — call 740-3339 for information.

For information on the Toronto ferry to Centre Island, Ward's Island, and Hanlan's Point, call 392-8139.

GAY PLACES OF INTEREST

Toronto's gay and lesbian community is located on Church Street near Wellesley Street. Here you will find many gay owned and operated businesses, including bars, restaurants, and the new home of *Xtra!*, Toronto's biweekly gay and lesbian newspaper.

The 519 Community Centre, located at 519 Church Street, is the local gay and lesbian community centre. Give them a call at 392-6874 for information on many lesbian and gay events. Behind "the 519" is Cawthra Park. In the summer, Cawthra Park is often referred to as "Cawthra Beach," due to the many scantily clad gay men found soaking up the sun.

Gay Pride Day is usually celebrated on the last Sunday in June, but this year will be observed on July 2. The Gay Pride Day Parade is one of Toronto's largest and most flamboyant parades, with last year's attendance estimated at 700,000! It is a colourful display of gay and lesbian visibility, complete with theme floats and music. Gay Pride Day is officially recognized in Toronto.

ENTERTAINMENT

Although there is a wide range of gay establishments to visit in Toronto, the city also has an abundance of mainstream sights to take in.

Some of the more traditional sites to visit include: the CN Tower (Toronto's most famous, tallest phallic symbol located at Union Station, at 301 Front Street West); Skydome (a magnificent mound opposite the CN Tower. Its claim to fame is its retractable domed roof, as well as being home to the Toronto Blue Jays baseball team); the CNE, or Exhibition Place (open during the last three weeks in August, the "Ex" is a Toronto fun tradition); Ontario Place (home of the Cinesphere, which is a giant movie screen with special educational films); the Eaton Centre (Toronto's largest shopping mall, which extends from Queen Street to Dundas, along Yonge Street); AGO (the Art Gallery of Ontario at 317 Dundas Street West); ROM (the Royal Ontario Museum, located at 100 Queen's Park. This has recently been remodelled, and it has one of the best dinosaur exhibits and Egyptian exhibits); Roy Thomson Hall (the acoustics are fabulous — Liza Minnelli said so herself — located at 60 Simcoe Street); Casa Loma (a real castle in the middle of Toronto at 1 Austin Terrace and you can be queen for a day. Daily tours are available. Call 923-1171); Black Creek Pioneer Village (located at 100 Murray Ross Parkway); Canada's Wonderland (located just minutes north of Toronto. Call 832-7000 extension 8100); Metro Toronto Zoo (it is open year round. Call 392-5900); Ontario Science Centre (at 770 Don Mills Road. Call 696-3127. There are lots of buttons to push).

If camping is your thing, try Buddies in Bad Times Theatre, at its dazzling new Alexander Street location. In April, Buddies sponsors QueerCulture, and in February it is the host of Rhubarb! — a festival of experimental lesbian and gay theatre.

Shopping in T.O. is to die for, especially along the "Golden Mile," situated on Bloor Street between Yonge Street and Avenue Road. There is also fabulous shopping to be had in the underground shopping malls, and in the Eaton Centre.

CRUISING AREAS

Toronto has many hot cruising spots to check out. Try the popular Hanlan's Point located west of Centre Island. To get there take the Toronto Island Ferry, of course.

Cherry Beach is a gay spot at the foot of Cherry Street, which is four blocks east of Parliament Street.

Kew Beach, at the foot of Woodbine Avenue offers some good cruising.

During the summer months, try going to Cawthra Beach, located behind the 519 Community Centre, on Church Street.

High Park is also a prime cruising area, but be careful around this area.

At the corner of Carlton and Sherbourne Streets is Allan Gardens, where you can look at the flowers and pluck some daisies while you're at it.

Another prime cruising area is David Balfour Park, where the hills are alive, but not with the sound of music, especially in the evenings during the summer months in the wooded areas.

Queen's Park is located north of the Ontario parliament buildings, and the cruising area of Philosopher's Walk is found one block west and just north of Queen's Park.

The steps outside the Second Cup at Church and Wellesley are always a good place to sit and watch the gays walk by.

THE DYKE DISTRICT

Although there is a proliferation of gay bars, Toronto offers surprisingly little for its lustful lesbians. There is now only one bar specifically for lesbians, called The Rose, located at 547 Parliament Street, south of Wellesley Street. There is a $5.00 cover charge on Saturday nights.

Tallulah's Cabaret, located at Buddies in Bad Times Theatre, offers a night for lesbians called "Viva Vulva," on Friday nights, for which there is no cover charge.

Also on Friday nights is "Bent Night," held at the Catch 22 (379 Adelaide Street West, call 369-1583). It is primarily a straight bar that offers this night for lesbians, bisexuals, and gay men, and there is a $5.00 cover charge. Try out Sistah's Café on Queen Street West, too.

Toronto, Ontario (416)

ACCOMMODATION/BED & BREAKFAST

Acorn House Bed & Breakfast

255 Donlands Ave., M4J 3R5

PHONE: 463-8274

Receive that little extra personal touch at Acorn House B&B, where you'll stay in a clean, bright, comfortable room, in a private home with a beautiful garden. Just a 10-minute walk from Greektown and 15 minutes by subway to downtown Toronto and the gay and lesbian establishments. Reservations are required.

The proprietor is Jeff Schmidt.

RATES: $30 to $50

HOURS: Daily 8:00 a.m. – 10:00 p.m.

PAYMENT: cash, cheques

▼ ⚣ ⚢

Allenby Guest Suites

223 Strathmore Blvd., M4J 1P4

PHONE: 461-7095

Fully furnished suites available for short-term or long-term stays.

▽ ⚤

Amblecote Bed & Breakfast

109 Walmer Rd., M5R 2X8

PHONE: 927-1713

Rambling historic home, superbly located near tourist attractions and downtown core. Enjoy Edwardian elegance and the pleasures of an earlier time. Guests are invited to make use of the Steinway grand piano or simply sit in one of the cosy inglenooks with a good book. There is a cat and dog in residence. Non-smoking. E-mail: amblecote@interlog.com.

RATES: $55 to $65

PAYMENT: cash, personal and traveller's cheques, MasterCard, VISA

▼ ⚤

Beverley Place
235 Beverley St., M5T 1Z4
PHONE: 977-0077, FAX: 920-3922
Beverley Place is within easy walking distance of all major gay attractions and facilities.
RATES: $45 to $65 singles, $60 to $85 doubles
PAYMENT: cash (preferred), traveller's cheques, American Express, MasterCard, VISA
▽ ⚥

Burken Guest House
322 Palmerston Blvd., M6G 2N6
PHONE: 920-7842, FAX: 960-9529
Quiet, stately home, furnished with antiques and located on tree-lined street. Close to TTC, non-smoking, continental breakfast, parking, telephones, ceiling fans, clock-radios, private sinks, and shared bathrooms.
RATES: $45 to $55 single
$60 to $65 double
$75 triple
PAYMENT: cash, traveller's cheques, MasterCard, VISA
▼ ⚥

Catnaps 1892 Downtown Guest House
246 Sherbourne St., M5A 2S1
PHONE: 968-2323, FAX: 413-0485
Toll-free: 1-800-205-3694
Catnaps is a bed & breakfast located in downtown Toronto, steps from the nightlife, restaurants, shopping, tourist attractions, and theatres. Friendly service, fresh-baked continental breakfast, and clean rooms with comfortable lodgings at reasonable rates.
RATES: $37 to $60
PAYMENT: cash, personal and traveller's cheques, MasterCard, VISA
▽ ⚣ ⚢

Hotel Selby — Boots & The Kurbash
592 Sherbourne St., M4X 1L4
PHONE: 921-3142, FAX: 923-3177
Toll-free: 1-800-387-4788
Victorian-style hotel with 67 rooms. Toronto's largest gay complex on premises — three bars, a disco, a courtyard, live entertainment, and hotel

guests have health club and kitchen privileges. On-site laundry and limited day parking.

RATES: From $49.95
Suites from $99.95

HOURS: Daily 24 hours.

PAYMENT: cash, American Express, MasterCard, VISA

▼ ⚥

Mike's on Mutual
333 Mutual St., M4Y 1X6
PHONE: 944-2611

This is an older home in the heart of Toronto's gay village. Two rooms share a bath. No smoking in this home. Open year-round. This is a bed & breakfast.

RATES: $50 single
$65 double

PAYMENT: cash, cheques, VISA

▼ ⚣ ⚢

Muther's Guest House above the Toolbox
508 Eastern Ave., M4M 1C5
PHONE: 466-8616

Laid-back guest house with comfortable rooms above a men's leather bar. No disco floor, so noise is never a problem. The restaurant in Toolbox serves full meals as well as pub grub. Reservations are preferred. Only partially wheelchair accessible. A leather and adult toy shop on the premises.

RATES: $45 to $60 weekends
$30 to $45 Weeknights

▼ ⚣

Rosedale Ritz
c/o Michael Pearl
30 Elm Ave, Apt. 314, M4W 1N5
PHONE: 920-9227

Seaton Pretty Bed & Breakfast
327 Seaton St., M5A 2T6
PHONE: 972-1485

RATES: $55 single
$65 double
$85 coach house

PAYMENT: cash, traveller's cheques

▼ ⚥

Badlands/Neighbours/K Factory
9 Isabella St., M4Y 1M7
PHONE: 960-1200
Lesbian and gay country bar, full-service restaurant open until 10:00 p.m. with Sunday brunch at 11:00 a.m. One thousand square feet for line dancing and two-stepping. Wheelchair accessible only downstairs. K Factory is a high-energy dance bar upstairs.
▽ ⚣ ⚢

Bar 501
501 Church St., M4Y 2C6
PHONE: 944-3272, FAX: 968-7669
Neighbourhood bar located in the heart of the Church-Wellesley area. Rotating art shows featuring local artists on the walls. Weekly events, pleasant atmosphere, great street view through windows open to Church Street.
♿ ▼ ⚣ ⚢

The Barn/Stables
418 Church St., M5B 2A3
PHONE: 977-4702

Bijou XXX
370 Church St., M5B 2A2
PHONE: 960-1272
HOURS: Daily 9:00 p.m. – 4:00 a.m.
[*Editor's note*: New. Two screens and a licensed bar. Bar closes at 1:00 a.m. and there is a $5 entry fee.]

Black Eagle
459 Church St., M4Y 1C5
PHONE: 413-1219
Leather cruise bar. This includes denim, uniforms, rubber, and fetish. Finger foods are served. On Thursday to Saturday, the dress code is strictly enforced — no running shoes or casualwear and no drag.
HOURS: Monday to Friday 4:00 p.m. – 2:30 a.m.
Saturday and Sunday 2:00 p.m. – 2:30 a.m.
▼ ⚣

Boots/The Kurbash
592 Sherbourne St., M4X 1L4
PHONE: 921-0665, FAX: 923-3177
Toll-free: 1-800-387-4788
Boots has Toronto's largest dance bar and showroom. The Kurbash is Toronto's newest exotic playroom. Year-round courtyard.
HOURS: Daily noon – 1:00 a.m.
PAYMENT: cash, MasterCard, VISA
♿ ▼ ⚥

Club Bolero
2261 Dundas St. W., M6R 1X6
PHONE: 533-2628
[*Editor's note*: Latin gays and lesbians.]

Club Generations
1 Isabella St., M4Y 1M7
PHONE: 962-5895

Colby's/Stage II
5 – 9 St. Joseph St., M4Y 1J6
PHONE: 961-0777
▼ ⚥

Crews
508 Church St., M4Y 2C8
PHONE: 972-1662

El Convento Rico
750 College St., M6G 1C4
PHONE: 588-7800

Fantasies
699 Yonge St., 2nd floor, M4Y 2B2
PHONE: 968-2832
[*Editor's note*: Presents "Heavens" (968-2832 ext. 9) on Sunday nights. Hot male dancers. Use entrance on Charles St.]

Keith's Sports Bar & Grill
619 Yonge St., 2nd floor, M4Y 1Z5
PHONE: 922-3068

The Living Well Restaurant and Bar Upstairs
(See entry under RESTAURANTS/CAFÉS heading.)

My Treehouse
485 Church St., M4Y 2C6
PHONE: 926-8780

Pegasus Billiard Lounge
491 Church St., #201, M4Y 2C6
PHONE: 927-8832
▼ ⚥

Pints Restaurant & Pub
518 Church St., M4Y 2C8
PHONE: 921-8142

Playground
7 St. Joseph St., M4Y 1J6
[*Editor's note*: This is a bar/dark room. No number listed.]

Pockets Bar 'N Grill
545 Yonge St., M4Y 1Y5
PHONE: 968-POOL, FAX: 968-9426
▽ ⚥

Remington's (Men of Steel)
379 Yonge St., M5B 1S1
PHONE: 977-2160, FAX: 924-7506
Male strip club, featuring 70 naked male strippers. Two stages and two bars.
▼ ⚣

Rhino's Bar & Restaurant

1249 Queen St. W., M6K 1L5
PHONE: 535-8089
[*Editor's note*: Wednesday nights for gays and lesbians.]

The Rose Café

547 Parliament St., M4X 1P7
PHONE: 928-1495
[*Editor's note*: Lesbian only.]
⚢

Sailor

465 Church St., M4Y 2C5
PHONE: 975-8899
The look and feel of a turn-of-the-century ocean liner. Sailor attracts the hottest men in the city. There is a stand-up and sit-down bar with a live D.J., a pool table, and pinball. Weekend brunch and lunch daily.
HOURS: Daily noon – 1:00 a.m.
PAYMENT: cash, traveller's cheques, American Express, MasterCard, VISA
♿ ▽ ⚣ ⚢

Stud Bar

488 Church St., M4Y 1X5
PHONE: 516-8087
Operates on Thursday and Friday nights.
▼ ⚣

The Toolbox

(See Muther's under ACCOMMODATION/BED & BREAKFAST heading.)
Men's leather bar with restaurant on the premises. Pool table, video/pinball games, large outdoor patio.

Trax V — Purple Tiger Inc.

529 Yonge St., M4Y 1Y5
PHONE: 963-5196

Woody's

467 Church St., M4Y 2C5
PHONE: 972-0887
A neighbourhood bar in the heart of "Boystown," Woody's features one of Toronto's busiest nightclubs and after-work scenes. There is a D.J., but no dance floor. Friendly staff, eclectic decor, a famous weekend brunch, and Toronto's hottest men.

HOURS: Monday to Friday noon – 1:00 a.m.
Saturday and Sunday 11:00 a.m. – 1:00 a.m.
PAYMENT: cash, traveller's cheques, American Express, MasterCard, VISA
▽ ⚣ ⚢

Zoo Bar
526 Queen St. W., M5V 2B4
PHONE: 777-9453, FAX: 777-2697
▽ ⚥

BATHS/SAUNAS

The Barracks
56 Widmer St., M5V 2E9
PHONE: 593-0499
Bath for leather men. Steam room, dry sauna, and fantasy rooms.
HOURS: Daily 24 hours
PAYMENT: cash, VISA
▼ ⚣

The Cellar
78 Wellesley St. E., M4Y 1H2
PHONE: 944-3779
Machine recording describes atmosphere as subterranean and very dark. There is no number on the door — it's just a big black door.
HOURS: Daily 24 hours

Club Toronto
231 Mutual St., M5B 2B4
PHONE: 977-4629, FAX: 698-7952
Open 24 hours, outdoor pool, Sunday buffet or BBQ by the pool. Twenty years of service to the gay community.
HOURS: Daily 24 hours
PAYMENT: cash, traveller's cheques
▼ ⚣

Oak Leaf Steam Baths
216 Bathurst St., M5T 2R9
PHONE: 368-2424

The St. Marc Spa
543 Yonge St, 4th floor, M4Y 1Y5
PHONE: 927-0210, FAX: 927-9203
PAYMENT: cash, traveller's cheques, American Express
♿ ▼ ⚣

The Spa on Maitland
66 Maitland St., M4Y 1C5
PHONE: 925-1571
Large comfortable rooms, in and out privileges for out-of-town guests, TV lounge, video lounge, large gym, and licensed to sell beer and alcohol.
HOURS: Daily 24 hours
PAYMENT: cash, VISA
▼ ⚣

BOOKSHOPS/LIBRARIES

Another Story
261 Danforth Ave., M4K 1N2
PHONE: 462-1104
Queer issues section, as well as anti-racist material, labour issues, international fiction, and children's books.
HOURS: Monday to Friday 11:00 a.m. – 7:00 p.m.
Saturday 9:30 a.m. – 7:00 p.m.
Sunday 11:00 a.m. – 6:00 p.m.
▽ ⚥

Bob Miller Bookroom
180 Bloor St. W., Lower Concourse, M5S 2V6
PHONE: 922-3557

Canadian Lesbian and Gay Archives
(See listing under MUSEUMS/ARCHIVES heading.)

Common Knowledge Books
602 Markham St., M6G 2L8
PHONE: 539-8550, FAX: 539-8587
Cultural issues, gender issues, healing, and spirituality. Large gay and lesbian section. This store specializes in non-fiction.
♿ ▽ ⚥

David Mirvish Books
596 Markham St., M6G 2L8
PHONE: 531-9975, FAX: 531-5543

Ex Libris
583 Church St., 2nd floor, M4Y 2E4
PHONE: 962-8660
[*Editor's note*: Used gay and lesbian books.]
▼ ⚦

The Glad Day Bookshop
598A Yonge St., M4Y 1Z3
PHONE: 961-4161, FAX: 961-1624
Toronto's only specifically gay and lesbian bookshop. Over nine thousand titles currently in print in fiction and non-fiction. In business for over 24 years. Newsletter is printed every month and mail orders are accepted.
HOURS: Monday to Friday 10:00 a.m. – 9:00 p.m.
Saturday 10:00 a.m. – 7:30 p.m.
Sunday (and holidays) noon – 6:00 p.m.
PAYMENT: cash, personal and traveller's cheques, money orders, U.S. money at going exchange rate, American Express, MasterCard, VISA
▼ ⚣ ⚢

Longhouse Bookshop
497 Bloor St. W., M5S 1Y2
PHONE: 921-0389, FAX: 921-8614
[*Editor's note*: Sells specifically Canadian books.]

The Omega Centre Bookstore
29 Yorkville Ave., M4W 1L1
PHONE: 975-9086, FAX: 975-0731
A bookstore devoted to self-discovery offering over 10,000 titles from astrology to zen and everything in between. Mail orders accepted.
HOURS: Monday to Friday 10:00 a.m. – 9:00 p.m.
Saturday 10:00 a.m. – 6:00 p.m., Sunday 11:00 a.m. – 5:00 p.m.
PAYMENT: cash, personal and traveller's cheques, MasterCard, VISA
♿ ▽ ⚦

100th Monkey Books
66 Wellesley St. E., 2nd floor, M4Y 1G2
PHONE: 925-7633
[*Editor's note*: Sells new-age books.]

Pages
256 Queen St. W., M5V 1Z8
PHONE: 598-1447, FAX: 598-2042

Parentbooks
201 Harbord St., M5S 1H6
PHONE: 537-8334, FAX: 537-9499
Books on pregnancy, childbirth, health education, and social sciences. Mail orders accepted.
HOURS: Monday to Saturday 10:30 a.m. – 6:00 p.m.
PAYMENT: cash, personal and traveller's cheques, MasterCard, VISA
▽ ⚧

That Other Bookstore
17 Hayden St., M4Y 2P2
PHONE: 966-1483, FAX: 966-2748
Toll-free: 1-800-668-BOOK
TradeNet: 783-4684 (computer on-line shopping)
HOURS: Monday to Wednesday 10:00 a.m. – 7:00 p.m.
Thursday and Friday 10:00 a.m. – 9:00 p.m.
Saturday 11:00 a.m. – 6:00 p.m.

This Ain't the Rosedale Library
483 Church St., M4Y 2C6
PHONE: 929-9912

Toronto Women's Bookstore
73 Harbord St., M5S 1G4
PHONE: 922-8744, FAX: 922-1417
The Toronto Women's Bookstore is a non-profit feminist bookstore and a cultural service, serving as a forum for a wide range of perspectives on women's issues and experiences. Exceptional selection of women's books, music, jewellery, posters, journals, magazines, and safe-sex products. Mail orders are accepted. Only the first floor is wheelchair accessible.
HOURS: Monday to Thursday, Saturday 10:30 a.m. – 6:00 p.m.
Friday 10:30 a.m. – 7:00 p.m.
Closed Sundays except in December
PAYMENT: cash, personal and traveller's cheques, MasterCard, VISA
▼ ⚢ ♀ ⚤

Volumes Bookstore
74 Front St. E., Market Square, M5E 1T4
PHONE: 366-9522
General bookshop with a section of gay and lesbian books.
HOURS: Monday, Wednesday, Thursday 10:00 a.m. – 6:00 p.m.
Tuesday 10:00 a.m. – 9:00 p.m.
Friday 10:00 a.m. – 9:30 p.m.
Saturday 9:30 a.m. – 9:30 p.m.
▽ ⚤

CHURCHES/RELIGIOUS ORGANIZATIONS

Christos Metropolitan Community Church
353 Sherbourne St., M5A 2S3
PHONE: 925-7924
Christos MCC is a Christian church with a special welcome for members of the lesbian and gay communities. Members gather from a wide variety of spiritual backgrounds to worship God and to care for each other.
HOURS: Monday to Friday 1:30 p.m. – 5:00 p.m.
Thursday service: 6:30 p.m.
Sunday service: 7:00 p.m. and 9:30 p.m.
♿ ▼ ⚤

Integrity Toronto
P.O. Box 873, Station F, M4Y 2N9
PHONE: (905) 273-9860

An Anglican ministry to and by lesbians and gay men and their friends.
PAYMENT: cheques
♿ ▼ ⚥

Lutherans Concerned
Contact: Lionel Johnston
PHONE: 588-9399

Metropolitan Community Church of Toronto
115 Simpson Ave., M4K 1A1
PHONE: 406-6228, FAX: 466-5207
HOURS: Sunday service: 11:00 a.m. and 7:00 p.m.
PAYMENT: cash, personal and traveller's cheques, MasterCard, VISA
♿ ▼ ⚣ ⚢

GALLERIES

A Space
183 Bathurst St., M5T 2R7
PHONE: 364-3227, FAX: 360-0781
A multi-disciplinary art centre featuring community-based and politically engaged programming. The gallery welcomes proposals from individual artists, groups, and curators, particularly those from diverse cultural backgrounds. The Gallery newsletter, *Appendum*, is published about four times yearly and encourages the submission of articles from the community.
HOURS: Tuesday to Friday 11:00 a.m. – 6:00 p.m.
Saturday noon – 5:00 p.m.
PAYMENT: cash, cheques
▽ ⚥

O'Connor: A Gallery
473A Church St., M4Y 2C5
PHONE: 921-7149
[*Editor's note*: New gay and lesbian art gallery.]
▼ ⚣ ⚢

Women's Art Resource Centre (WARC)
80 Spadina Ave., Suite 506, M5V 2J3
PHONE: 861-0074, FAX: 861-1441
WARC houses a library of books, periodicals, and an artist's file/slide registry representing over nine hundred practising Canadian women artists. WARC sponsors lectures, workshops, open portfolio nights, and showcases women

artists represented in the registry through The Walls of Warc exhibition program. *Matriart: A Canadian Feminist Art Journal* is published by WARC.
♿ ▽ ⚤

HEALTH CLUBS

Bloor Valley Club
555 Sherbourne St., M4X 1W6
PHONE: 961-4695
⚤

Village Green Fitness Club
60 Alexander St., M4Y 1B4
PHONE: 922-1197
HOURS: Monday to Saturday 6:00 a.m. – 10:00 p.m.
Sunday 7:00 a.m. – 6:00 p.m.
⚣

YMCA
20 Grosvenor St., M4Y 1A8
PHONE: 975-9622, FAX: 324-4222

MUSEUMS/ARCHIVES

Canadian Lesbian and Gay Archives
201 – 56 Temperance St.
Mailing address: Box 639, Station A, M5W 1G2
PHONE: 777-2755
The CLGA is a non-profit, charitable research library and archive devoted to documenting lesbian and gay life, past and present, in all media. A superb collection of lesbian and gay Canadiana and the largest collection of gay/lesbian periodicals in the world. Ask for a copy of the newsletter, *Lesbian and Gay Archivist.*
HOURS: Tuesday to Thursday 7:30 p.m. – 10:00 p.m.
(and by appointment)
PAYMENT: cash, personal and traveller's cheques
♿ ▼ ⚤

Women's Art Resource Centre
(See listing under GALLERIES heading.)

The Canadian Lesbian and Gay Archives

An archives, library, and research centre, founded in 1973, dedicated to the recovery and preservation of lesbian, gay, and bisexual histories.

HOURS: Tuesday, Wednesday, and Thursday, 7:30 – 10:00 p.m., or by appointment

LOCATION: 56 Temperance Street, Ste. 201
Toronto, Ontario

ADDRESS: P.O. Box 639, Station A
Toronto, Ontario M5W 1G2

The Boudoir Noir
P.O. Box 5, Station F, M4Y 2L4
PHONE: 591-2387, FAX: 591-1572
Bimonthly non-fiction magazine about the leather/fetish/consensual S&M scene in North America. Photos, articles, reviews, news, and a calendar. A sample copy is $10 and a six-issue subscription is $24.
PAYMENT: cash, personal and traveller's cheques
▽ ⚥

CENTRE/FOLD
(See entry for Toronto Centre for Lesbian and Gay Studies under OTHER.)

Fab Magazine
25 Wood St., Suite 104, M4Y 2P9
PHONE: 599-9273, FAX: 599-0964
Ontario's gay life-style and information source.
HOURS: Monday to Friday 9:00 a.m. – 5:00 p.m.
PAYMENT: cash, personal cheques
▼ ⚣

Fireweed: A Feminist Quarterly
P.O. Box 279, Station B, M5T 2W2
PHONE: 504-1339
An eclectic and lively journal, *Fireweed* is available at gay, feminist, progressive, and alternative bookstores. Call or write for submission guidelines or subscription information.
PAYMENT: cash, cheques
⚢ ♀

Icon
P.O. Box 459, Station P, M5S 2S9
PHONE: 537-7387
[*Editor's note*: Monthly gay/lesbian magazine.]

Lickerish
24 Noble St., #105, M6K 2C8

Pink Pages
392 King St. E., M5A 1K9
PHONE: 864-9132, FAX: 861-0174
[*Editor's note*: Free annual guide to Toronto.]

Sorority Magazine
P.O. Box 57, 1170 Bay St., M5S 2B4
Published by, for, and about gay women, this 96-page quarterly life-style magazine is packed with fiction, profiles, feature articles, and reports from the worlds of art, entertainment, and literature along with photographs, cartoons, puzzles and more.
PAYMENT: money orders only
▼ ⚢

Xtra!
491 Church St., Suite 200, M4Y 2C6
PHONE: 925-6665, FAX: 925-6674
Toll-free: 1-800-268-XTRA
Other numbers: Tel-A-Guide 925-XTRA (24-hr touch-tone guide to Toronto's gay community)
The gay and lesbian biweekly for Toronto and surrounding area.
HOURS: Daily 24 hours
PAYMENT: cash, personal and traveller's cheques, money orders, MasterCard, VISA
▼ ⚣ ⚢

RESTAURANTS/CAFÉS

Bemelman's Restaurant & Bar
83 Bloor St. W., M5S 1M1
PHONE: 960-0306

The Berkeley Café
141 Berkeley St., M5A 2X1
PHONE: 603-9791
A comfortable little neighbourhood café with patio in spring/summer. Serving specialty salads and sandwiches, Middle Eastern cuisine, and lots on the grill. Fully licensed.
▽ ⚤

Bulldog Café/457 Restaurant
457 Church St., M4Y 2C5
PHONE: 923-3469
▼

PHOTO: RANIER ELSTERMANN OF POP AGAINST HOMOPHOBIA
sorority magazine
A 96 page lifestyle quarterly packed with fiction, profiles, features (on relationships, politics, athletics and health) and reports from the worlds of art, entertainment and literature along with photographs, cartoons, puzzles and more!
Current issue $ 5.95
A year subscription (mailed) $ 24.95
Suite 110 ▲ 1170 Bay Street
Toronto, Ontario ▲ Canada M5S 2B4

Byzantium
499 Church St., M4Y 2C6
PHONE: 922-3859, FAX: 920-9949
Twenty-seat bar, gold-medal design-award winner in 1992. Elegant restaurant serving the finest in eastern Mediterranean food. Washroom not wheelchair accessible. Reservations recommended.
HOURS: Monday to Saturday 5:00 p.m. – 1:00 a.m.
Sunday noon – midnight
▽ ⚧

Café Volo
587 Yonge St., M4Y 1Z4
PHONE: 928-0008

Coffee Café
5 Isabella St., M4Y 1M7
PHONE: 961-2414
Now celebrating its sixth year. The Coffee Café must be regarded as Toronto's unique coffee experience. Its colourful cast of regulars has created a family atmosphere, mixing working class with working girls. Open round the clock, the Coffee Café has become a gathering place for Toronto's most eclectic individuals, be it breakfast, bartime, or bedtime.
▽ ⚧

Devon Restaurant
556 Church St., M4Y 2E3
PHONE: 921-4121, FAX: 921-3579

The Diner
9 Isabella St., M4Y 1M7
PHONE: 960-1200

Hernando's Hideaway
545 Yonge St., M4Y 1Y5
PHONE: 929-3629

L'Echalote Restaurant
51 St. Nicholas St., M4Y 1W6
PHONE: 921-9226
Fine French cuisine steps away from the gay community.
Reservations are required. Fully licensed.

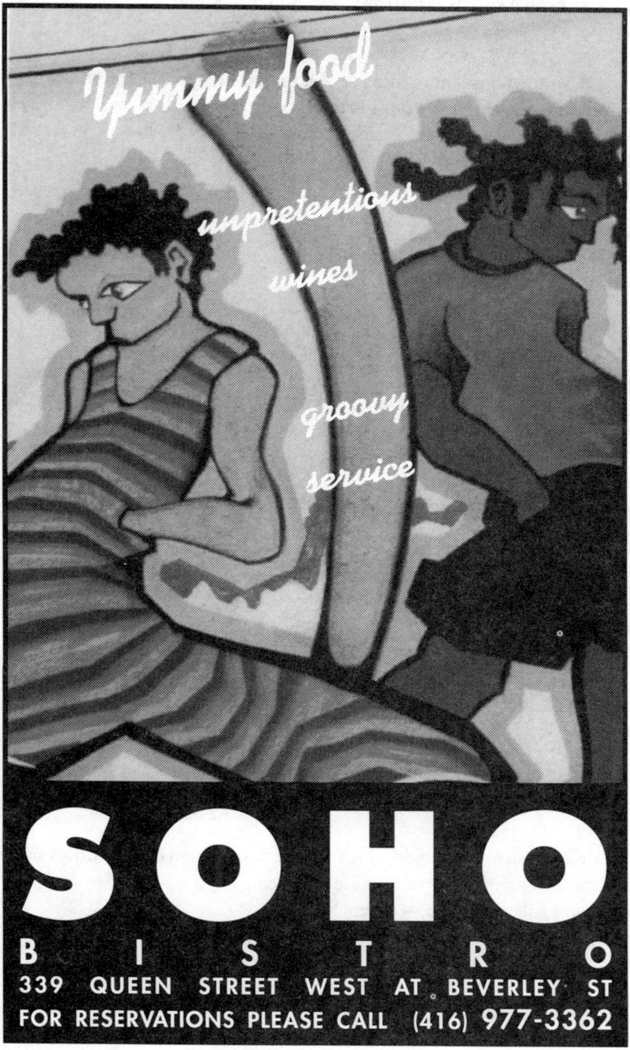
Yummy food
unpretentious
wines
groovy
service
SOHO
B I S T R O
339 QUEEN STREET WEST AT BEVERLEY ST
FOR RESERVATIONS PLEASE CALL (416) 977-3362

The Living Well Restaurant and Upstairs Bar
692 Yonge St., M4Y 2A6
PHONE: 922-6770, FAX: 922-0396
Busy downtown restaurant and bar. All food is homemade and the kitchen is open late. Comfortable relaxed atmosphere, reasonably priced. In business for over 13 years. Serving mainly continental cuisine, pastas, vegetarian dishes, Thai, and desserts.
♿ ▽ ⚣ ⚢

Mammina's Ristorante
6B Wellesley St. W., M4Y 1E7
PHONE: 967-7199

Mango
580 Church St., M4Y 2E5
PHONE: 922-6525
Creative cuisine, cozy atmosphere.
▼ ⚥

Mocha Joe's
399 Church St., M5B 2J6
PHONE: 971-6356, FAX: 979-7779

Pam's Coffee & Tea Co.
585 Church St., M4Y 2E4
PHONE: 923-7267

Pints Restaurant & Bar
518 Church St., M4Y 2C8
PHONE: 921-8142

P.J. Mellons Restaurant
489 Church St., M4Y 2C6
PHONE: 966-3241
P.J. Mellons is a fully licensed wine restaurant, offering a menu with a variety of classy dishes. No reservations are required.
HOURS: Daily 11:00 a.m. – midnight
PAYMENT: cash, traveller's cheques, American Express, MasterCard, VISA
▽ ⚥

Queen Mother Café
208 Queen St. W., M5V 1Z2
PHONE: 598-4719 (office: 977-5082), FAX: 977-5082

Established in 1978. Famous for authentic Lao-Thai cuisine and sinful desserts at affordable prices. Its garden patio offers sanctuary from urbanitis.
HOURS: Monday to Saturday 11:30 a.m. – 1:00 a.m.
PAYMENT: cash, traveller's cheques, American Express, MasterCard, VISA
♿ ▽ ⚥

Rhino's Bar & Restaurant
1249 Queen St. W., M6K 1L5
PHONE: 535-8089

The Rivoli
332 Queen St. W., M5V 2A2
PHONE: 597-0794 (office: 977-5082), FAX: 977-5082
Under one roof: a restaurant with spectacular dishes, a lounge/bar with great cocktails, a live-venue club with varied entertainment, a pool hall with thirteen antique tables, and a sidewalk café with a view of the Queen Street parade. Serving Asian/Caribbean cuisine.
HOURS: Daily 11:30 a.m. – 1:00 a.m.
PAYMENT: cash, traveller's cheques, American Express, MasterCard, VISA
▽ ⚥

Rockit
120 Church St., M5C 2G8
PHONE: 947-9555, FAX: 947-9319

Second Cup
516 Church St., M4Y 2E1
PHONE: 960-6301
HOURS: Daily 24 hours
♿ ⚥

Sistah's Café
1080 1/2 Queen St. W., M4M 1K5
PHONE: 532-9642

Soho Bistro
339 Queen St. W., M5V 2A4
PHONE: 977-3362, FAX: 924-8493
Soho Bistro is conveniently located in the heart of Toronto's trendy fashion district in the heart of the Queen West Village. All entrees are prepared from the finest and freshest ingredients.
HOURS: Monday to Friday 11:00 a.m. – 3:00 p.m./5:00 p.m. – 11:00 p.m.
Saturday 11:00 a.m. – 11:00 p.m., Sunday 5:00 p.m. – 11:00 p.m.

PAYMENT: cash, En Route, Diners Club, Carte Blanche, traveller's cheques, American Express, MasterCard, VISA

▼ ⚧

Toby's
542 Church St., M4Y 2E1
PHONE: 929-0411

Treehouse Café
485 Church St., M4Y 2C6
PHONE: 926-8780

Unicorn Family Restaurant
477 Church St., M4Y 2C6
PHONE: 961-0616

Vagara Bistro
475 Church St., M4Y 2L5
PHONE: 964-0403

RETAIL

Allure Lingerie
357 1/2 Yonge St., M5B 1S1
PHONE: 597-3953
Allure Lingerie provides a large assortment of adult toys and love oils. Allure also carries erotic lingerie, exotic leather, and stilettos, in addition to cards, novelties, videos, and magazines.
HOURS: Monday to Saturday 10:00 a.m. – 9:00 p.m.
Sunday noon – 6:00 p.m.
PAYMENT: cash, traveller's cheques, American Express, MasterCard, VISA

▽ ⚧

Amnesia
551 Church St., M4Y 2E2
PHONE: 925-5009

Binding Leather
44 Dovercourt Rd., M6J 3C3
PHONE: 533-6042

Cinéma Bleu Inc.

12 Roy's Square, M4Y 2W2
PHONE: 944-9112, FAX: 944-8612
An erotica shop specializing in new releases and the best in adult video. A comfortable upscale boutique located at the centre of downtown, within walking distance of all gay restaurants and bars. Great toy shop!
♿ ▼ ⚤

Doc's Leathers and Harley Davidson Gear/ Doc's Vintage Records

562 Parliament St., 2nd floor, M4X 1P8
PHONE: 324-8686/961-7399, FAX: 929-1849
Jackets, jocks, leather toys, boots, chaps, restraints, caps, hoods, custom-designed items, electrical apparatus, alterations and drycleaning. Ten percent off for cash. Doc's also sells vintage records, CD's, vinyl, tapes, rare recordings, memorabilia, and cool stuff.
HOURS: Daily 11:00 a.m. – 11:00 p.m.
PAYMENT: cash
▼ ⚣ ⚢

Flatiron's Giftstore

449 Church St., M4Y 2C5
PHONE: 968-9274

Leathercraft

606 Yonge St., M4Y 1Z3
PHONE: 924-5018, FAX: 975-1337
Manufacturer and retailer of leatherwear and clubwear. Custom work done on the premises.
♿ ▽ ⚤

Lee's Glitz

455 Church St., M4Y 2C5
PHONE: 975-1343
Over 40,000 of the most unique cards to select from, for every occasion. The most creative supplies, ideas, and staff to help with all your party needs. Committed to the ongoing fight against AIDS!
♿ ▽ ⚤

Mineral Gallery

562 Parliament St., M4X 1P8
PHONE: 968-6682, FAX: 929-1849
Rocks, fossils, gifts in minerals, gemstones, bones, skulls, sculptures, pen-

dants, obelisks, spheres, geodes, crystals, pyramids. The rare and unusual. Five to 10 percent off with cash.
HOURS: Daily 11:00 a.m. – 7:00 p.m.
PAYMENT: cash
▼ ⚥

Neat Stuff
475 Parliament St., M5A 3A3
PHONE: 928-0132
▽ ⚥

New Release Adult Video
489 Church St., lower level, M4Y 2C6
PHONE: 966-9815

Northbound Leather Ltd.
19 St. Nicholas St., M4Y 1W5
PHONE: 972-1037, FAX: 975-1337
Canada's fetish embassy. Realize the fantasy. Manufacturer and retailer of leather, latex, PVC, stilettos, corsets, restraints, body jewellery, and much more. Also sells books and magazines.
Two catalogues — one for leather and latex clothing, the other for bondage gear and access toys.
♿ ▽ ⚥

Out on the Street Inc.
551 Church St., M4Y 2E2
PHONE: 967-2759, FAX: 967-0224
Toll-free: 1-800-263-5747
Canada's friendly neighbourhood queer store. A catalogue is available and mail orders are accepted.
HOURS: Daily, various hours
PAYMENT: cash, traveller's cheques, American Express, MasterCard, VISA
▼ ⚣ ⚢

Paradise Gym
117 Danforth Ave., M4K 1N2
PHONE: 466-6202

Priape
465 Church St., M4Y 2C5
PHONE: 586-9914, FAX: 586-0212
Toll-free: 1-800-461-6969

Founded in 1974, Priape is Canada's gay store selling books, mags, videos, leather, sexy clothing, and accessories. Catalogue available and mail orders accepted.

▼ ⚣ ⚢

Rubyfruit Erotica
P.O. Box 386, Station P, M5S 2S9
[*Editor's note*: Write and request catalogue.]

Significant Other Designs
481A Church St., M4Y 2C6
PHONE: 944-2021

Studio Auroboros
580 Yonge St., M4Y 1Z3
PHONE: 962-7499
Bodypiercing and custom jewellery.
HOURS: Tuesday to Saturday noon – 8:00 p.m.
▽ ⚥

Sweet Sensation
505 Yonge St., M4Y 1Y4
PHONE: 925-9008
Sweet Sensation provides a large selection of adult toys and love oils, as well as a wide variety of exotic leather, sexy lingerie, stilettos, cards (gay and lesbian), videos, and magazines.
HOURS: Monday to Saturday 10:00 a.m. – 9:00 p.m.
Sunday noon – 6:00 p.m.
PAYMENT: cash, traveller's cheques, American Express, MasterCard, VISA
▽ ⚥

Uprise Gifts
483 1/2 Church St., M4Y 2C6
PHONE: 968-2037
Uprise is the only specialty condom shop on Church Street (in the heart of the gay community). Also specializes in a variety of unique gift items and greeting cards, as well as newly released CDs. The stock is constantly changing to cater to the diverse and distinguished tastes of people in the community.
▼ ⚣ ⚢

AIDS Committee of Toronto (ACT)

399 Church St., M5B 2J6
PHONE: 340-2437, FAX: 340-8224
Hotline: 340-8844
The AIDS Committee of Toronto is Canada's largest AIDS service organization and has the largest AIDS-related resource library. Services available include counselling, support groups, community education, and practical help for those affected by HIV/AIDS.
HOURS: Monday to Thursday 10:00 a.m. – 9:00 p.m.
Friday 10:00 a.m. – 5:00 p.m.
♿ ▼ ⚥

Canadian Lesbian and Gay Archives

(See MUSEUMS/ARCHIVES heading.)

The 519 Church Street Community Centre

519 Church St., M4Y 2C9
PHONE: 392-6874
The 519 Community Centre provides a wide range of services to its downtown Toronto neighbourhood. Community information includes information on lesbian and gay community services and groups.
HOURS: Monday to Friday 9:00 a.m. – 10:30 p.m.
Saturday noon – 6:00 p.m.
Sunday 10:00 a.m. – 5:00 p.m.
PAYMENT: cash, cheques
♿ ▽ ⚥

Parents-FLAG

Contact: Carroll Austin-Jewitt
PHONE: 322-0600
Meets the first Wednesday and third Friday of every month. Call for meeting location.

Toronto Area Gay/Lesbian Phone Line (TAGL)

PHONE: 964-6600
HOURS: Monday to Saturday 7:00 p.m. – 10:00 p.m.

TRAVEL/TOURS

Canadian Adventure Tours

255 Donlands Ave., M4J 3R5
PHONE: 463-8274
For your personalized holiday in Ontario. Offers everything from city of Toronto tours to day trips to Niagara Falls, as well as 14-day Ontario tours in English or German. Write or phone for a brochure.
RATES: Depends on type of tour taken.
HOURS: Daily 8:00 a.m. – 10:00 p.m.
PAYMENT: cash, cheques
▼ ⚣ ⚢

Escape Travel

469 Church St., M4Y 2C5
PHONE: 962-4833, FAX: 962-4101
Full-service travel agency which specializes in gay and lesbian travel, events, and services.
▼ ⚥

Exta Sea Sailing

PHONE: 948-1506 (Skipper: Philip Fotheringham)
[*Editor's note*: Toronto sailing cruises from April to October. The phone number was temporarily disconnected when we called. It may only be in use during the April – October time period.]

La Fabula Travel & Tours

551 Church St., M4Y 2E2
PHONE: 920-3229
▼ ⚣ ⚢ ⚥

Masters in Travel

104 – 33 Isabella St., M4Y 2P7
PHONE: 922-2422

Talk of the Town Travel

565 Sherbourne St., M4X 1W7
PHONE: 960-1393, FAX: 960-6379
Full service IATA registered travel agency.
PAYMENT: cash, MasterCard, VISA

The Travel Clinic (a division of Jeeves Travel)
506 Church St., M4Y 2C8
PHONE: 962-2242, FAX: 962-6621
Toll-free: 1-800-387-1240
Full-service, IATA-registered travel agency offering complete range of professional travel services to lesbians and gay men, across Canada. Call for more information.
♿ ▼ ⚤

Village Vacations
204 – 65 Wellesley St. E., M4Y 1G7
PHONE: 929-2000, FAX: 929-8331
An entire resort exclusively for gay men and women.
▼ ⚣ ⚢

OTHER

Buddies in Bad Times Theatre
12 Alexander St., M4Y 1B4
PHONE: 975-8555, FAX: 975-9293
World's largest lesbian/gay and innovative theatre. An artist-run, non-profit, queer theatre company committed to the development and production of radical new Canadian work. As a pro-sexual company, we celebrate difference and challenge the professional theatre experience by blurring and reinventing boundaries between: artistic disciplines, performer and audience, gay and lesbian, and queer and straight.
♿ ▼ ⚤

Gaywire CIUT
89.5 FM
PHONE: 595-0909, FAX: 595-5604

Pink Antenna/Queer Noises
CKLN 88.1 FM
PHONE: 595-1477, FAX: 595-0226
HOURS: Pink Antenna: Tuesdays 7:00 p.m. – 8:00 p.m.
Queer Noises: Wednesdays 11:00 a.m. – 2:00 p.m.

Toronto Centre for Lesbian and Gay Studies (TCLGS)
100 – 129 2 Bloor St. W., M4W 3E2
PHONE: 925-9872, ext. 2810
E-mail: ejackson@inforamp.net
The TCLGS is an independent, community-based organization that sponsors publications, events, and research promoting a critical understanding of queer lives, histories, and cultures. Membership in the Centre, which includes a subscription to the newsletter *CENTRE/FOLD*, is $25 regular, $10 student/unwaged.
PAYMENT: cheques
▼ ⚣ ⚢

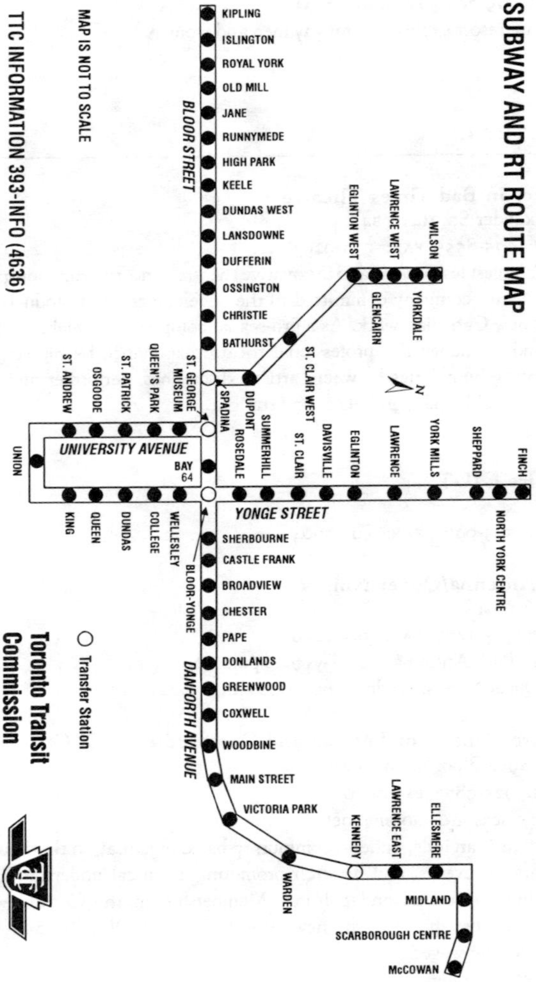
SUBWAY AND RT ROUTE MAP
MAP IS NOT TO SCALE
TTC INFORMATION 393-INFO (4636)
KIPLING
ISLINGTON
ROYAL YORK
OLD MILL
JANE
RUNNYMEDE
HIGH PARK
KEELE
DUNDAS WEST
LANSDOWNE
DUFFERIN
OSSINGTON
CHRISTIE
BATHURST
BLOOR STREET
ST. GEORGE
SPADINA
DUPONT
ST. CLAIR WEST
EGLINTON WEST
GLENCAIRN
LAWRENCE WEST
YORKDALE
WILSON
N
MUSEUM
QUEEN'S PARK
ST. PATRICK
OSGOODE
ST. ANDREW
UNION
UNIVERSITY AVENUE
BAY
64
KING
QUEEN
DUNDAS
COLLEGE
WELLESLEY
BLOOR-YONGE
ROSEDALE
SUMMERHILL
ST. CLAIR
DAVISVILLE
EGLINTON
LAWRENCE
YORK MILLS
SHEPPARD
NORTH YORK CENTRE
FINCH
YONGE STREET
SHERBOURNE
CASTLE FRANK
BROADVIEW
CHESTER
PAPE
DONLANDS
GREENWOOD
COXWELL
WOODBINE
DANFORTH AVENUE
MAIN STREET
VICTORIA PARK
WARDEN
KENNEDY
LAWRENCE EAST
ELLESMERE
MIDLAND
SCARBOROUGH CENTRE
McCOWAN
Transfer Station
Toronto Transit Commission

Women's Press
233 – 517 College St., M6G 4A2
PHONE: 921-2425, FAX: 921-4428
Women's Press is Canada's oldest and largest English-language feminist book publisher. Publishes lesbian fiction, poetry, plays, and anthologies, as well as books for children of lesbians. Focuses on Canadian authors and international writers. Submissions from women of colour are welcomed. A catalogue is available and mail orders are accepted.
HOURS: Monday to Friday 10:00 a.m. – 5:00 p.m.
PAYMENT: cash, cheques, MasterCard, VISA
♿ ▽ ⚢ ♀

Waterdown, Ontario (905)

ACCOMMODATION/BED & BREAKFAST

Cedar's Tent & Trailer Park
1039 – 5th Concession W., L0R 2H0
Mailing address: Box 195, Milgrove, Ontario L0R 1V0
PHONE: 659-3655
This campground is 130 acres with a clubhouse, pool, mini-putt golf course, volleyball, softball, restaurant, laundry room, and dances. Some trailer rentals available. Open May through to September.
PAYMENT: cash, cheques
♿ ▽ ⚣ ⚢

Windsor, Ontario (519)

BARS

Club Happy Tap Tavern
1056 Wyandotte St. E., N9A 3K3
PHONE: 256-8998

JB's Bar & Grill
1880 Wyandotte St. E., N8Y 1E3
PHONE: 258-5706
Casual, friendly atmosphere in an old house. Bar serves Friday night dinner parties (5:00 p.m. – 11:00 p.m.) and Sunday brunch (11:00 a.m. – 3:00 p.m.).
HOURS: Monday to Saturday 4:00 p.m. – 1:00 a.m.
Sunday 11:00 a.m. – 1:00 a.m.
PAYMENT: cash, traveller's cheques, MasterCard, VISA
▼ ⚥

BATHS/SAUNAS

Vesuvio Steam Bath
563 Brant St., N9A 3E5
PHONE: 977-8578

CHURCHES/RELIGIOUS ORGANIZATIONS

Metropolitan Community Church of Windsor
P.O. Box 2052, N8Y 4R5
PHONE: 977-6897
MCC of Windsor worships Sundays at 3301 Edison. Phone number is an answering machine for evening events.
HOURS: Sunday service is at 10:30 a.m.
♿ ⚥

PUBLICATIONS

One in Ten
P.O. Box 2233, N8Y 4R8
PHONE: c/o AIDS Committee 973-0222
[*Editor's note*: By and for youth.]

SERVICES

AIDS Committee

2090 Wyandotte St. E.
OR: P.O. Box 2233, N8Y 4R8
PHONE: 973-0222
HOURS: Monday to Friday 9:00 a.m. – 5:00 p.m.

Windsor Gayline

PHONE: 973-4951
HOURS: Monday nights for women 8:00 p.m. – 10:00 p.m.
Thursday and Friday nights for men 8:00 p.m. – 10:00 p.m.
Wednesday nights for youth 7:00 p.m. – 9:00 p.m.

Province of Québec

Québec is a province of distinct cultures. The primary language of Québec is French, although English is spoken to a large degree in Montréal, due to its large anglo population, as well as to the number of English-speaking visitors this architecturally beautiful city attracts.

There is a large gay and lesbian presence in Québec, found mainly in Montréal, and, to a smaller degree, in Québec City.

The province of Québec has its own anti-discrimination laws protecting gays and lesbians. That, along with the "laissez-faire" attitude so prevalent in the province, finds gays and lesbians in Québec fairly free to enjoy themselves.

This does not mean that gay bashing is unheard of; it is, however, not committed on the same scale as in other, less tolerant areas of Canada.

Québec's Provincial Sales Tax is 8 percent, with a special 4 percent only on accommodations. The legal drinking age is 18.

Acton Vale, Québec (514)

ACCOMMODATION/BED & BREAKFAST

Domaine Plein Vent Inc.
Box 101, J0H 1A0
PHONE: 549-5831

Chicoutimi, Québec (418)

BARS

Au Vieux Pub
460 Racine E., G7H 1T7
PHONE: 543-7454

Drummondville, Québec (819)

BARS

Resto-Bar Idem
1895 Mercure, J2B 3N9
PHONE: 477-0988
HOURS: Wednesday to Sunday 3:00 p.m. – 3:00 a.m.
PAYMENT: cash, traveller's cheques, MasterCard, VISA
♿ ▼ ⚣ ⚢

Joliette, Québec (514)

ACCOMMODATION/BED & BREAKFAST

L'Oasis des Pins
381 Brassard, J0K 3E0
PHONE: 754-3819
Open from April to September.

Jonquière, Québec (418)

BARS

Le Café-Bar
2171 St. Dominique, G7X 6M8
PHONE: 547-6934

Lac des Plages, Québec (819)

ACCOMMODATION/BED & BREAKFAST

L'Auvent Bleu
6 Vendée, JOT 1KO
PHONE: 687-2981, FAX: 687-2722
Comfortable country home in the Laurentian Mountains, situated on the banks of the Maskinonge River. Sit back and relax in the peaceful atmosphere and country surroundings. Full breakfast. Please reserve.
RATES: $35 single
$55 double
PAYMENT: cash, MasterCard
▼ ⚤

Longueil, Québec (514)

BATHS/SAUNAS

Sauna 1286
1286 Chambly, J4J 3W6
PHONE: 677-1286

Sauna Rive-Sud Inc.
945 Boul. Taschereau, J4K 2X2
PHONE: 677-2349
▼ ⚣ ⚥

CHURCHES/RELIGIOUS ORGANIZATIONS

Église Communauté du Village
321 Lafayette, J4K 3A1
PHONE: 679-9362
Sundays at 7:30 p.m. at 1212 Panet, room 204.

Mont-Tremblant, Québec (819)

ACCOMMODATION/BED & BREAKFAST

Versant Ouest
110 LaBelle, JOT 1Z0
PHONE/FAX: 425-6615
Toll-free: 1-800-425-6615
Versant Ouest is an elegant country house in the Laurentians, one and a half hours from Montreal. Five minutes from Tremblant Station.
RATES: $56 to $60 single
$75 to $80 double
PAYMENT: cash, traveller's cheques, MasterCard
▼ ⚣ ⚢

MONTRÉAL: *A Brief Description*

Add romance, beauty, history, cultural diversity, a strong lesbian and gay presence, and you have Montréal.

Founded by the French in 1642 on the Huron Indian site of Hochelaga, the city became an important fur-trading post. In 1759, the British took over the city. Today, only about one fifth of the city's population is English, with the majority being French. There is also a large population of Italians, Ukrainians and Germans inhabiting the city. Montréal also boasts the largest Jewish population in Canada.

VISITING MONTRÉAL

For visitor information:
Info-Touristique (150-page guide) available at 1001 Dorchester Square (between Peel and Metcalfe).
PHONE: (514) 873-2015

Winters in Montréal are long, snowy, and cold. The summer months are hot, and in the cruising areas (see CRUISING AREAS for more information) it gets even hotter.

GETTING AROUND MONTRÉAL

Northwest of Montréal is Mirabel International Airport, and southwest of the city lies Dorval International Airport.

The Trans-Canada highway, along with more than 10 other major highways, makes driving into Montréal quick and easy.

Major streets traversing the city include Métropolitain Boulevard, Sherbrooke, and Notre-Dame Streets.

Montréal boasts an efficient and inexpensive public transit system, with a single adult ticket costing $1.75. We highly recommend this system for travelling around the city. The Métro, Montréal's subway, operates from 5:30 a.m until 1:00 a.m. Buses on major streets run all night long.

Taxis are easily flagged on main streets, and are available at all hours.

GAY PLACES OF INTEREST

Montréal has bustling gay and lesbian communities, with many restaurants, bars, and stores to visit. See Montréal's listing of gay and lesbian establishments for more information.

Since 1993, gays and lesbians in Montréal have celebrated Gay Pride Day on August 1. This was done to avoid having their day of pride overshadowed by the province's observation of St. Jean Baptiste Day, which is a national holiday in Québec.

ENTERTAINMENT

Montréal is a renowned cultural centre, with a veritable menagerie of events to experience.

At Sherbrooke and Drummond Streets you will find the Montréal Museum of Fine Arts. The world-famous Place des Arts, home of the Montréal Opera, is located at Ste. Catherine and St. Urbain (pronounced urban) Streets.

For romantic overtures, visit the Montréal Symphony, and for fans of dance, waltz over to Les Feux-Follets or Les Grands Ballets Canadiens, both in downtown Montréal. Experience the French culture to the fullest, and see plays performed in the French language at Le Theatre du Nouveau Monde and Le Theatre du Rideau-Vert.

Summer offers a wide range of exciting events. The visually spectacular International Fireworks Festival is held from late May until late June. Zoom off to the Canadian Grand Prix in mid-June, and swing over to Montréal's International Jazz Festival held in late June until early July. And, of course, attend the mardi-gras-style party of St. Jean Baptiste Day, Québec's national holiday, on June 24.

Late September sees Le Grand Prix cycliste des Ameriques, a 200-kilometre (125-mile) bicycle race. All those form-fitting spandex shorts will really get you working up a sweat.

If you like to go down, ski Mount Royal or in the beautiful, nearby Laurentian Mountains. And nothing sounds more exciting than skating on Beaver Lake in Mount Royal Park.

For those were prefer to do it in the dark, attend the gay and lesbian film and video festival, in November.

Visit L'Androgyne, Montréal's lesbian and gay bookstore, for the most recent lesbian and gay titles.

CRUISING AREAS

There are quite a few spots for cruising, but don't forget that there are police around, so be careful. Also, parks are closed to the public between midnight and 6:00 a.m., and if the police find you in one, you will be charged and fined. You can cruise Lafontaine Park, bordered by Sherbrooke, Rachel, Papineau, and Parc Lafontaine Streets (get off at Sherbrooke Metro station). The best time to cruise this centrally located park is in the evening, with the most action happening near the pathways that wind along two artificial lagoons. There has, however, been a lot of police harassment here lately.

Another good area is Mount Royal Park, along the mountain's eastern slope. To get there, get off at Mont-Royal Metro station. The best spots are the foot paths in the wooded areas. Montréal's only mounted police force patrols this park, and the police have also increased security around this area recently, so exercise caution.

Around Metro Beaudry, in the gay village, is also a prime cruising spot. The gay village is located below Ontario Street, between Amherst and Papineau, near many of Montreal's gay baths and saunas, making this a particularly hot cruising area.

If you stay around Amherst and Papineau in the gay village region of Ste.

Catherine Street, you won't be disappointed with all of the spectacular sights in this cruising spot.

The Complexe Desjardins, at the Place-des-Arts Metro stop, is another prime cruising area. It is a shopping mall with many restaurants, bars, and boutiques, and is linked with the Place des Arts and the Museum of Contemporary Arts.

Square Dorchester, formerly known as Dominion Square, is located between Peel and Metcalfe Streets, at Peel Metro station. It is a small, centrally located park, with many monuments.

Other good cruising spots are Carré St. Louis, and Main railway station.

Maisonneuve Park, at Viau Metro station, is also a popular park for cruising. For more park cruising, there are Baldwin, Jarry, and Stanley Parks.

The strip along Tupper Street, near the Montréal Forum, is a popular cruising area. The Place Alexis-Nihon, a shopping mall at Atwater Metro station, also offers some good action. Public washrooms are not recommended, mostly due to increased police surveillance, and increased cases of entrapment.

THE DYKE DISTRICT

On St. Denis Street, north of Sherbrooke, lies the dyke district. You'll find quite a few lesbian and mixed bars here, and several guest houses specifically for women travellers.

There are many cafés and restaurants with a large women's following, located in both the gay village and lesbian districts. Also found along St. Denis Street are many bistros and outdoor cafés, and there's nothing like enjoying a café au lait on the oh-so-gay St. Denis strip!

Montréal, Québec (514)

ACCOMMODATION/BED & BREAKFAST

Au Bon Vivant Guesthouse
1648 Amherst, H2L 3L5
PHONE: 525-7744, FAX: 525-2874
Perfectly located featuring three guest rooms with shared bathrooms. Warm colours, fine furnishings, and Persian carpets make this fine home your private home in Montréal.

RATES: May to October $50 to $75, November to April $44 to $64
PAYMENT: cash, traveller's cheques, American Express, MasterCard, VISA
▼ ⚣ ⚢

Aux Berges
1070 MacKay, H3G 2H1
PHONE: 938-9393, FAX: 938-1616
Aux Berges is an all-male hotel with fifty rooms. Downtown Montreal with standard comfort, sauna, sundeck, bar-terrace. They consider themselves to be a large family and welcome you to join them.
▼ ⚣

Bed & Breakfast du Village (BBV)
1279 Montcalm, H2L 3G6
PHONE: 522-4771
Two beautiful houses located in the centre of the gay village of Montréal, with 14 rooms and one bachelor pad. The staff and very reasonable rates make it a good choice when staying in Montréal. Reservations are required and there is free parking.
▼ ⚣

Bistro-Auberge l'un et l'autre
1641 Amherst, H2L 3L4
PHONE: 597-0878, FAX: 597-1430
Located in the gay village, this accommodation also has a restaurant/bar that serves fine French food. Reservations are usually required.
♿ ▼ ⚣ ⚢

La Chasseur Guesthouse
1567 St. André, H2L 3T5
PHONE: 521-2238

Chateau Cherrier
550 Cherrier, H2L 1H3
PHONE: 844-0055, FAX: 844-8438
Toll-free: 1-800-816-0055
First-class B&B. Magnificent Tudor-style house. Located downtown and walking distance from the gay village. Delicious full breakfast prepared by Chef Léo. Free private parking. Please make a reservation.
RATES: $50 to $75
PAYMENT: cash, traveller's cheques, American Express, MasterCard, VISA
▼ ⚣ ⚢

La Conciergerie Guest House
1019 St. Hubert, H2L 3Y3
PHONE: 289-9297, FAX: 289-0845
Montréal's finest offers 17 comfortable rooms with a choice of shared or private baths, air conditioner, European breakfast, jacuzzi, rooftop sundeck, and a terrific location. See for yourself why they come highly recommended.
RATES: $52 to $118
PAYMENT: cash, traveller's cheques, American Express, Diner's, MasterCard, VISA
▼ ⚣ ⚢

Days Inn — Old Montréal
1199 Berri, H2L 4C6
PHONE: 845-9236, FAX: 849-9855
Toll-free: 1-800-363-0363
Days Inn is convenient to Montréal's business and cultural centres, located only steps away from the celebrated cafés, bars, boutiques, and theatres of famous St. Denis Street. The Days Inn offers quality at affordable prices. The restaurant serves Italian and continental cuisine (Restaurant Il Cavaliere).
RATES: Low season $83, High season $89
(specials available during both seasons)
PAYMENT: cash, traveller's cheques, American Express, Diner's/EnRoute, Discover, MasterCard, VISA
♿ ▽ ⚤

La Douillette Bed & Breakfast
7235 de Lorimier, H2E 2N9
PHONE: 376-2183
Come in and relax at la Douillette, located near the subway. It offers a warm and friendly atmosphere complete with homemade jams, small garden, and purring cat. Women only. Bienvenue!
RATES: $40 to $60
PAYMENT: cash, traveller's cheques
▼ ⚢

Hotel Pierre
169 Sherbrooke, H2X 1C7
PHONE: 288-8519
L'Hotel Pierre est situé au coeur des activités touristique, prix affordable et un service expérimenté pour un client exigeant. Les groupes sont bienvenues. Reservations are required.
▼ ⚥

Hotel Le Saint-Andre
1285 St. André, H2L 3T1
PHONE: 849-7070, FAX: 849-8167
Hotel Le Saint-Andre is a small, European-style accommodation. All rooms have a private bath, TV/radio, air conditioning, and a continental breakfast is served every morning.
RATES: starting at $46.50
▽ ⚦

Hotel Le Bourbon
1574 Ste. Catherine E., H2L 2J2
PHONE/FAX: 523-4679, *Toll-free*: 1-800-268-4679
Gay and lesbian hotel in the heart of Montreal's gay village. All rooms are equiped with a bathroom, mini-bar, and television.
▼ ⚣ ⚢

Lindsey's B&B for Women
3974 Laval Ave., H2W 2J2
PHONE: 843-4869
⚢ ♀

Maison Chablis Hotel/Bar/Restaurant
1639 – 1641 St. Hubert, H2L 3Z1
PHONE: 523-0053, FAX: 596-1519
Friendly ambiance in a renovated Victorian row house with spacious rooms and eclectic decor. Two terraces, a sundeck, and two large eat-in kitchens. Continental breakfast, modest rates, conveniently situated above the famous Chablis restaurant.
▼ ⚣ ⚢

Le Stade Bed & Breakfast
P.O. Box 42-A, Station M, H1V 3L6
PHONE: 254-1250
An accommodation for travellers from around the world. Clean, bright, and large rooms in a residential area. Close to all public transport and 10 minutes to the gay village. Call for a flyer.
RATES: $55 to $95 in season, $30 to $70 off season
Rates may change, so call first.
HOURS: Daily 24 hours
PAYMENT: cash, personal cheques (conditions apply), traveller's cheques (not over $20)
▼ ⚣ ⚢

Le St. Christophe Bed & Breakfast
1597 St. Christophe, H2L 3W7
PHONE: 527-7836
All-male guest house, one block from rue Ste. Catherine. Five antique-furnished guest rooms, full breakfast, jacuzzi, and working fireplace are just some of our amenities.
⚣

La Tourquoise Bed & Breakfast
1576 Alexandre-de-Seve, H2L 2V7
PHONE: 523-4679

Vallieres Bed & Breakfast
6562 de Lorimier, H2G 2P6
PHONE: 729-9552
⚢

BARS

L'Adonis
1681 Ste. Catherine E., H2L 2J5
PHONE: 521-1355
[*Editor's note*: Male strip bar.]
⚣

Angora
1160 MacKay, H3G 2H4
PHONE: 939-1976
⚣

Bar Aigle Noir/Black Eagle Bar
1315 Ste. Catherine E., H2L 2H4
PHONE: 529-0040
Cruising bar with videos and a pool table.

Dallas Montréal
2490 Mont Royal E., H2H 1L3
PHONE: 598-1351
Country bar.
HOURS: Thursday to Saturday 7:00 p.m. – 3:00 a.m.
⚣

L'Exit II
4297 St. Denis, H2J 2K9
PHONE: 843-8696
⚢

Factory 1278
1278 St. André, H2L 3S9
PHONE: 842-1336

Harlinda
16 Ontario E., H2X 3W2
PHONE: 288-3463
⚢

L'Idem
1669 Ste. Catherine E., H2L 2J5
PHONE: 597-0814
⚢ ⚣

Katakombes / Sis♀ers / K.O.X.
1450 Ste. Catherine E., H2L 2H8
PHONE: 523-0064
⚣ ⚢

Lézard
4177 St. Denis, 2nd floor, H2W 2M7
PHONE: 289-9819
⚣ ⚢

Le Loubar
1364 Ste. Catherine E., H2L 2H6
PHONE: 523-9325, FAX: 523-4679
Toll-free: 1-800-268-4679
Lesbian bar in the heart of Montreal's gay village. Rooftop terrace.
HOURS: Thursday to Sunday 4:00 p.m. – 3:00 a.m.
PAYMENT: cash, traveller's cheques, American Express, MasterCard, VISA
▼ ⚢

Météorite
1665 Ste. Catherine E., H2L 2J5

Max
1166 Ste. Catherine E., H2L 2G7
PHONE: 598-5244

Packo Packo
451 Rachel E., H2J 2H1
PHONE: 499-0210

Playground
1296 Amherst, H2L 3K8
(enter through parking lot)
[*Editor's note*: After-hours bar. Cover charge of $10 after 2:00 a.m.]

Pub Taverne Terrasse du Village
1366 Ste. Catherine E., H2L 2H6
PHONE: 524-1960

Resto-Bar
1799 Amherst, H2L 3L7
PHONE: 528-7918

Robert Colby
1285 Amherst, H2L 3K9
[*Editor's note*: After-hours bar from 4:00 p.m. to 8:00 a.m., $5 cover after 2:30 a.m.]

Rocky I
1673 Ste. Catherine E., H2L 2J5
PHONE: 521-7865

Sky
1474 Ste. Catherine E., H2L 2J1
PHONE: 522-2475
⚣ ⚢

Taboo
1950 de Maissoneuve E., H2K 2C8
PHONE: 597-0010
[*Editor's note*: Male strip bar.]
⚣

Taverne Gambrinus
1151 Ontario, H2L 1R3
PHONE: 522-0416

Taverne le Plateau
71 Ste. Catherine E., H2X 1K5
PHONE: 843-6276

La Track
1584 Ste. Catherine E., H2L 2J2
PHONE: 523-4679
Toll-free: 1-800-268-4679
Montreal's busiest bar/tavern/disco. Great music and a large dance floor. Wednesday night is Woolco night and the beer is only $1.44.
HOURS: Daily 3:00 p.m. – 3:00 a.m.
PAYMENT: cash, traveller's cheques
♿ ▼ ⚣

BATHS/SAUNAS

Oasis Spa
1390 Ste. Catherine E., H2L 2H6
PHONE: 521-0785, FAX: 521-9849

Bain Sauna Centre-Ville Inc.
1465 Ste. Catherine E., H2L 2H9
PHONE: 524-3486, FAX: 442-3333
Number one in the village. Two floors, 60 rooms, lockers, hot tub, sauna, snack bar, movies, MuchMusic, air conditioned, and steam bath.
HOURS: Daily 24 hours
PAYMENT: cash, traveller's cheques (to $50), American Express, MasterCard, VISA
▽ ⚣

Sauna Bourbon
1574 Ste. Catherine E., H2L 2J2
PHONE/FAX: 523-4679

Sauna du Plateau
961 Rachel E., H2J 2J4
PHONE: 528-1679

Sauna 456
456 de la Gauchetière W., H2Z 1E3
PHONE: 871-8341, FAX: 871-1502
Large and hot. Entirely renovated. Great specials. Licensed.
HOURS: Daily 24 hours
PAYMENT: cash, traveller's cheques, MasterCard, VISA
▼ ⚣

Sauna 5018
5018 St. Laurent, H2T 1R7
PHONE: 277-3555

SSD
4109 St. Denis, H2W 2M7
PHONE: 289-9651

St. Marc
1168 Ste. Catherine E., H2L 2G7
PHONE: 525-8404

BOOKSHOPS/LIBRARIES

L'Androgyne Books
3636 St. Laurent, H2X 2V4
PHONE: 842-4765
Montréal's gay/lesbian/feminist bookstore. Books in English and French, magazines, music, and free catalogues. In operation for 21 years. Mail orders accepted.
HOURS: Monday to Wednesday 9:00 a.m. – 6:00 p.m.
Thursday and Friday 9:00 a.m. – 9:00 p.m.
Saturday and Sunday 9:00 a.m. – 6:00 p.m.
PAYMENT: cash, traveller's cheques, American Express, MasterCard, VISA
♿ ▼ ⚣ ⚢ ♀

Videomag Plus
1243 Bleury, H3B 3H9
PHONE: 871-1653, FAX: 871-8627
Videomag Plus specializes in adult videos and magazines. Some books. A catalogue is available and mail orders are accepted.
♿ ▽ ⚤

CHURCHES/RELIGIOUS ORGANIZATIONS

Dignity Montréal Dignité
P.O. Box 1045, Station H, H3G 2M9
PHONE: 398-9031
Gay and lesbian Catholics and friends meet the first and third Mondays of each month for worship, educational and social activities.
⚣ ⚢

HEALTH CLUBS

Physotech Plus
1657 Amherst, H2L 3L4
PHONE: 527-PLUS (7587)
Services offered: electro-muscle stimulation (EMS), sun-tanning beds, Swedish massage by professionals, flotation tank, skin-care treatments, waxing, and hairdressing. Mostly gay male.
HOURS: Monday to Friday 11:00 a.m. – 8:00 p.m.
Saturday 11:00 a.m. – 5:00 p.m.
▼ ⚣ ⚢

Stone Gym
1440 Ste. Catherine W., Faubourg Ste. Catherine, H3H 1L7
PHONE: 937-5061, FAX: 937-7370
Best gym in Montréal. Towel service. $12 per day or weekly price.
HOURS: Monday to Friday 6:30 a.m. – 10:30 p.m.
Weekends 8:00 a.m. – 8:00 p.m.
PAYMENT: cash, traveller's cheques, MasterCard, VISA
▼ ⚥

MUSEUMS/ARCHIVES

Archives Gaies du Québec
4067 St. Laurent, bur. 202, H2W 1Y7
Mailing address: C.P. 395, Succ. Place du Parc, H2W 2N9
PHONE: 287-9987
The Archives Gaies du Québec is a centre of documentation and reference, housing collections of manuscripts and printed documents, periodicals, posters, and photos pertaining to gay life in Québec and elsewhere.
HOURS: Thursday 7:30 p.m. – 9:30 p.m. or by appointment
PAYMENT: personal cheques
♿ ▼ ⚥

PUBLICATIONS

Attitude
617 St. Rémi, H4C 3G7
PHONE: 938-9585, FAX: 938-4635

Homo Sapiens
a/s ALGUQAM
C.P. 8888, Succ. A, H3C 3P8

Magazine Fugues
1212 St. Hubert, H2L 3H7
PHONE: 848-1854, FAX: 845-7645
Guide and news for the gay community — the most popular for 10 years. *Fugues* is published the last Thursday of every month. Le guide favori des gais depuis dix ans. *Fugues* est distribué gratuitement à travers la province.
▼ ⚣ ⚢

Magazine Gazelle
1212 St. Hubert, H2L 3H7
PHONE: 987-4992, FAX: 845-7645
Guide and news for the lesbian community, *Gazelle* is free. Available the last Thursday of every month. *Gazelle* est un guide et magazine pour lesbiennes, disponible le dernier jeudi du mois, gratuit.
HOURS: Daily 9:00 a.m. – 6:00 p.m.
PAYMENT: cash, cheques, VISA
▼ ⚢

Magazine RG
P.O. Box 5245, Station C, H2X 3M4
PHONE: 523-9463, FAX: 523-2214
Gay French magazine with news features. Erotic, social, and societal personals. Devoted to the defense of gay rights.
▽ ⚣ ⚢

Le Zipper
1212 St. Hubert, H2L 3Y7
PHONE: 848-1854, FAX: 845-7645
French erotic encounters.
HOURS: Daily 9:00 a.m. – 6:00 p.m.
PAYMENT: cash, traveller's cheques, MasterCard, VISA
▼ ⚣

RESTAURANTS/CAFÉS

L'Anecdote 1
801 Rachel E., H2G 2H7
PHONE: 526-7967

Après le Jour
901 Rachel E., H2J 2J2
PHONE: 527-4141, FAX: 527-4142 (phone first)

Binnerie du Village
2008 Amherst, H2L 3L8
PHONE: 525-1121

Bistro Quatre
4040 St. Laurent, H2W 1Y8
PHONE: 844-6246
[*Editor's note*: Women's night on Friday and Saturday.]

Cajun Restaurant
1574 Ste. Catherine E., H2L 2J2
PHONE/FAX: 523-4679

Café Clin d'Oeil
1429 de Maisonneuve E., H2R 1Z8
PHONE: 528-1209

Café L'Entre-Deux
4489 de la Roche, H2V 3V2
PHONE: 522-1616
European-style café. Posters and music from the fifties. Breakfast anytime, lunch, or dinner. Wine, croissant, salads, escargots, quiche, seafood, cheesecake, and fresh fruit.
HOURS: Daily 11:00 a.m. – 10:00 p.m.
PAYMENT: cash, MasterCard, VISA
♿ ▼ ⚥

Café Les Entretiens
1577 Laurier E., H2V 1V1
PHONE: 521-2934
Natural/healthy food. Licensed to sell beer and alcohol. In business for over 15 years. In the French heart of Montréal. Unique, warm, and non-discriminating.
HOURS: Daily 9:30 a.m. – midnight
PAYMENT: cash, traveller's cheques, MasterCard, VISA
♿ ▼ ⚥

Chablis Restaurant
(See Maison Chablis under ACCOMMODATION/BED & BREAKFAST heading)

Le Club Sandwich
1574 Ste. Catherine E., H2L 2J2
PHONE: 523-4679
Toll-free: 1-800-268-4679
Popular diner in the heart of Montréal's gay village. The place to eat breakfast and club sandwiches in a busy, active atmosphere.
HOURS: Daily 24 hours
PAYMENT: cash, traveller's cheques, American Express, MasterCard, VISA
♿ ▼ ⚦

La Fondue François
1256 Ontario, H2L 1R6
PHONE: 527-7639

La Paryse Snack-Bar
302 Ontario, H1Y 1H6
PHONE: 842-2040
Best hamburgers and fries in the warm ambiance of the fifties.
▽ ⚦

Le Pégase
1831 Gilford, H2H 1G6
PHONE: 522-0487
Cosy and warm atmosphere in a one-hundred-year-old house. Cuisine typical of southwest France. Not licensed — bring your own wine. Reservations required.
HOURS: Tuesday to Sunday 5:30 p.m. – 10:00 p.m.
PAYMENT: cash, traveller's cheques, MasterCard, VISA
▼ ⚦

Pizzadelic
1329 Ste. Catherine E., H2L 2H4
PHONE: 526-6011

Planet
1451 Ste. Catherine E., H2L 2H9
PHONE: 528-6953

Restaurant Chez Better
1310 de Maisonneuve E., H2L 2A4
PHONE: 525-9832
Restaurant specializing in European sausages and imported beers. Low prices in a bistro atmosphere, with a large terrace. They also serve German

specialties, and the best french fries.
♿ ▽ ⚥

Restaurant Napoléon
1694 Ste. Catherine E., H2L 2J4
PHONE: 523-2105

RETAIL

Basilic
1013 St. Hubert, H2L 3Y3
PHONE: 848-9581

Black Sun Studio Body Piercing
P.O. Box 1523, Place Bonaventure, H5A 1H6
PHONE: 345-5701
Private, appointment-only studio specializing in all types of exotic piercing and jewellery. Special services include piercings for sensual enhancement, chastity, enlarged piercings (tribal), custom-made jewellery, heavy-gauge jewellery, housecalls, ritual and "scene" piercings. Flexible hours.
PAYMENT: cash, personal and traveller's cheques
▽ ⚧

Body-Body
1326 Ste. Catherine E., H2L 2H5
PHONE: 523-0245

Choc
1881 Mont Royal E., H2H 1J3
PHONE: 521-7558

Cuir Plus/Leather Plus
1321 Ste. Catherine E., H2L 2H4
PHONE: 521-7587, FAX: 521-8046
Toll-free: 1-800-928-7587
First gay leather business in Canada and best quality and prices to be found. Ready-made and made-to-measure in store or via post. Also wholesale. Quality workmanship — attested to by customers from all over the world.
HOURS: Monday to Wednesday 10:00 a.m. – 6:00 p.m.
Thursday and Friday 10:00 a.m. – 9:00 p.m.
Saturday 10:00 a.m. – 5:00 p.m.
(open on long-weekend Sundays)

PAYMENT: cash, traveller's cheques, American Express, MasterCard, VISA

♿ ▼ ⚤

Erotim
818 Ste. Catherine E., H2L 2E2
PHONE: 982-2534

Fireboy (Men's Fitness Apparel)
C.P. 116, Succ. P.A.T., H1B 5K1
[*Editor's note*: Write for catalogue.]

Joe Blo
1412 de la Visitation, H2L 3B8
PHONE: 597-2330
Exclusive clothing and accessories from around the world.
HOURS: Monday to Wednesday noon – 6:00 p.m.
Thursday and Friday noon – 9:00 p.m.
Saturday noon – 5:00 p.m.
PAYMENT: cash, personal and traveller's cheques, MasterCard, VISA

♿ ▼ ⚤

Les Plaisirs d'Amour
1261 Bleury, H3B 3H9
PHONE: 392-1538, FAX: 871-8627
Fine and erotic lingerie. Gadgets. Mail orders are accepted.

♿ ▽ ⚤

Priape
1311 Ste. Catherine E., H2L 2H4
PHONE: 521-8451, FAX: 521-1309
Toll-free: 1-800-461-6969
Founded in 1974, Priape is Canada's gay store selling books, mags, videos, leather, sexy clothing, and accessories.
HOURS: Monday to Wednesday 10:00 a.m. – 6:00 p.m.
Thursday and Friday 10:00 a.m. – 9:00 p.m.
Saturday 11:00 a.m. – 5:00 p.m.
Sunday noon – 5:00 p.m.
PAYMENT: cash, traveller's cheques, INTERAC, American Express, MasterCard, VISA

▼ ⚣ ⚢

SERVICES

Canadian Accommodation Network

P.O. Box 42-A, Station M, H1V 3L6

PHONE: 254-1250

Serving gays and lesbians for over 10 years with worry-free room reservations, bar information, restaurant listings, plus local city maps and guides. Full-service network.

HOURS: Daily 24 hours

PAYMENT: depends on service

▼ ⚣ ⚢

Gayline (in English)

P.O. Box 384, Station H, H3G 2L1

PHONE: 990-1414

HOURS: Daily 6:30 p.m. – 10:00 p.m.

Gayline (in French)

PHONE: 521-1508

Lesbian/Gay Hospitality Exchange International (L/GHEI)

P.O. Box 612, Station C, H2L 4K5

FAX: 523-0806

An international non-profit membership network of lesbians and gay men willing to offer a couple of nights' hospitality to other members in exchange for being received when they travel.

PAYMENT: cash, personal and traveller's cheques, international and postal money orders

▼ ⚣ ⚢

M.A.N. (Male Accommodation Network)

2491 Centre, H3K 1J9

PHONE/FAX: 933-7571

Avoid the confusion of the guessing game. Free professional lodging reservation service for Montréal, Ottawa, Toronto, Niagara, and Québec. From a cosy pad to a luxurious jacuzzi suite, you'll choose from one extensive network of hotels, guesthouses, and bed & breakfasts — the accommodation that best suits your needs. Member IGTA. Deposit or credit card required.

RATES: vary

HOURS: Daily 9:00 a.m. – 10:00 p.m.

PAYMENT: cash, personal and traveller's cheques, VISA

▼ ⚣ ⚢

Montreal Gay & Lesbian Community Centre

2035 Amherst, H2L 3L9
Mailing address: C.P. 476, Succ. C, H2L 4K4
PHONE: 528-8424, FAX: 528-9708
Le centre offre un service de référence, d'animation sociale, des cours, un babillard communautaire, un journal, un centre de documentation, et un accueil chaleureux. The Centre offers different services: reference centre, social activities, courses, a quarterly newspaper, and a documentation centre in a warm environment.
HOURS: Monday to Friday 10:00 a.m. – 10:00 p.m.
♿ ▼ ⚣ ⚢

TRAVEL/TOURS

Alternative Travel

42 Pine W., Suite #2, H2W 1R1
PHONE: 845-7769, FAX: 845-8421, *Toll-free*: 1-800-267-7769

Club Voyages

920 de Maisonneuve E., H2L 1Z1
PHONE: 288-8688, FAX: 288-6259
In the heart of the gay village, Club Voyages offers destinations throughout the global village. Please request their calendar of events for the gay community. Au coeur du village, Club Voyages offre des destinations partout dans le village global. SVP consultez leur calendrier des evenements gais.
HOURS: Monday to Wednesday 9:00 a.m. – 6:00 p.m.
Thursday and Friday 9:00 a.m. – 8:00 p.m.
Saturday 11:00 a.m. – 5:00 p.m.
PAYMENT: cash, personal and traveller's cheques, American Express, Carte Blanche, Carte Bleue, Diner's, MasterCard, VISA
♿ ▼ ⚣

Gayroute

T-G-C c/o P.O. Box 1036, Station C, H2L 4V3
For information about business establishments of all types from any part of Canada, send a large self-addressed envelope and a list of your requests. Include $18 U.S. postal money order payable to cash. When you travel to Canada, use Gayroute as your guide. Send $2 U.S. for form/information to cover postage.
PAYMENT: cash
▼ ⚣ ⚢

Village Tours

2491 Centre, H3K 1J9

PHONE/FAX: 933-7571

An incoming receptive service company for groups planning a trip to eastern Canada (Québec and Ontario). They can help you prepare your group's itinerary, including lodging, restaurants, land transport, tour leaders, city tour guides, and activities.

▼ ⚣ ⚢

OTHER

Agence Flêche

P.O. Box 1036-E, Station C, H2L 4V3

PHONE: 521-7708

Over 10 years in operation. Escorts/companions, models, dancers. Clean, safe, and discreet. Special student rates.

HOURS: Daily 24 hours

PAYMENT: cash, traveller's cheques

▼ ⚣

CIBL 101.5 FM

HOURS: Saturday 3:30 p.m. – 4:30 p.m.

Tattoo*Club*Tatoue

P.O. Box 1036-T, Station C, H2L 4V3

A private and discreet club for men over 21 years of age who are tattooed or men who like men who are tattooed (nudists and couples welcome). Send a 4" x 6" photo of your tattoos.

▼ ⚣

Tropicales Massage

Box 1036-M, Station C, H2L 4V3

PHONE: 521-7708

Twelve years massage experience. California-style body rub. Aloe cream and tropical juices.

HOURS: Daily 24 hours

PAYMENT: cash, traveller's cheques

▼ ⚣

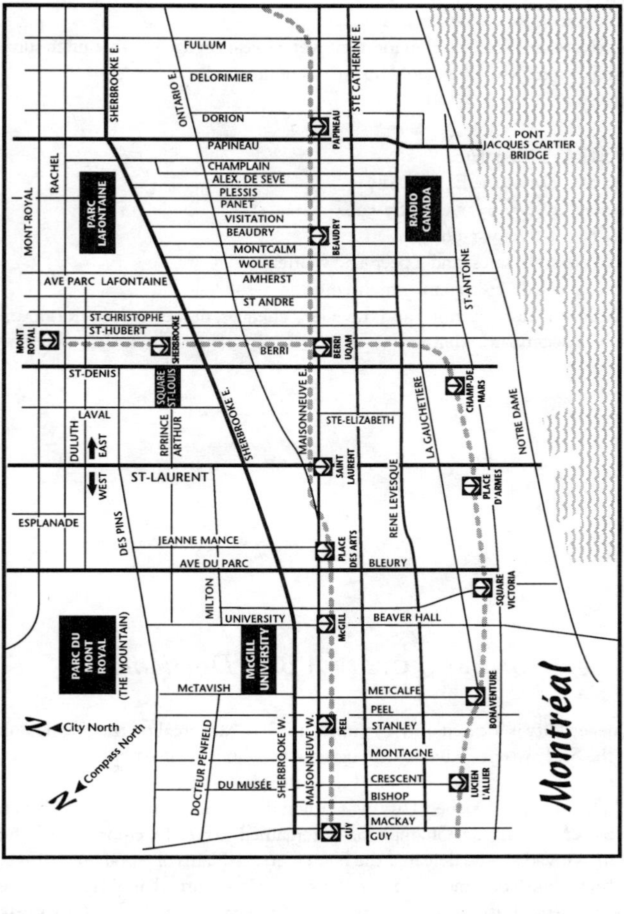
Montréal
FULLUM
DELORIMIER
DORION
PAPINEAU
CHAMPLAIN
ALEX. DE SEVE
PLESSIS
PANET
VISITATION
BEAUDRY
MONTCALM
WOLFE
AMHERST
ST ANDRE
ST-CHRISTOPHE
ST-HUBERT
BERRI
ST-DENIS
LAVAL
DULUTH
EAST
WEST
ST-LAURENT
ESPLANADE
DES PINS
JEANNE MANCE
AVE DU PARC
MILTON
UNIVERSITY
McTAVISH
DOCTEUR PENFIELD
DU MUSÉE
SHERBROOKE W.
MAISONNEUVE W.
SHERBROOKE E.
MAISONNEUVE E.
ONTARIO E.
STE CATHERINE E.
STE-ELIZABETH
BLEURY
BEAVER HALL
METCALFE
PEEL
STANLEY
MONTAGNE
CRESCENT
BISHOP
MACKAY
GUY
RENE LEVESQUE
LA GAUCHETIERE
ST-ANTOINE
NOTRE DAME
MONT-ROYAL
RACHEL
AVE PARC LAFONTAINE
PARC LAFONTAINE
SQUARE ST-LOUIS
RPRINCE ARTHUR
PARC DU MONT ROYAL
(THE MOUNTAIN)
McGILL UNIVERSITY
RADIO CANADA
PONT JACQUES CARTIER BRIDGE
PAPINEAU
BEAUDRY
BERRI UQAM
MONT ROYAL
SHERBROOKE
SAINT LAURENT
PLACE DES ARTS
McGILL
PEEL
GUY
CHAMP-DE-MARS
PLACE D'ARMES
SQUARE VICTORIA
BONAVENTURE
LUCIEN L'ALLIER
City North
Compass North

Uncut*Club*Prépuces Plus
P.O. Box 1036-U, Station C, H2L 4V3
A private and discreet club for men over 21 years of age who are uncircumcised or men who like men who are uncircumcised.
▼ ⚣

WEGA Video Inc.
930 Ste. Catherine E., H2L 2E7
PHONE: 987-5993, FAX: 987-5994
Toll-free: 1-800-361-9929
Video rentals, sales, and a peep-show cinema.
HOURS: Daily 10:00 a.m. – midnight
PAYMENT: cash, certified and traveller's cheques, money orders, INTERAC, MasterCard, VISA
♿ ▽ ⚥

QUÉBEC CITY: *A Brief Description*

Québec City is located only 157 miles north of Montréal on the north bank of the St. Lawrence River. Although the two cities are geographically close, their cultural development could not be further apart.

What is now Québec City was originally founded in 1608 by French explorer Samuel de Champlain. It remained a French colony until the British invaded, and defeated the French on the Plains of Abraham in 1759. While English became a prominent language in Montréal, it did not become so in Québec City, as today 95 percent of the people in Québec City speak French, and are of French origin.

Québec City is divided into two distinct sections, called upper town and lower town, connected by steep stairs and narrow streets. Upper town is surrounded by high walls, erected by the British in the early 1800s. Lower town is located on the edge of the river.

VISITING QUÉBEC CITY

For visitor information:

Tourisme Québec
P.O. Box 20000
Québec City, Québec G1K 7X2
PHONE: 1-800-363-7777
(9:00 a.m. – 5:00 p.m.)

The weather in Québec City is similar to that of Montréal, with very cold and snowy winters and hot, sunny summers.

GETTING AROUND QUÉBEC CITY

Due to its many steep staircases and narrow, winding streets, the easiest way to get around Québec City is on foot. You'll find many unique shops, and get an up-close and intimate view of this truly beautiful city.

GAY PLACES OF INTEREST

Québec City's gay bars are located around St. Jean Street, north of Place d'Youville. The gay scene is smaller and much more discreet than in Montréal. It is during Carnival time in February that the gay bars in Québec City are the busiest.

ENTERTAINMENT

Québec City hosts exciting events in both winter and summertime. The Québec International Summer Festival, held in the middle two weeks in July in Old Québec, is the largest French-speaking cultural event in North America. It includes many outdoor concerts and events, lots of them at no charge.

Winter brings, for two weeks in February, the city's world-famous Winter Carnival. People from the world over come to see the 11-day celebration, with snow sculpture competitions, nighttime parades, the canoe race across the St. Lawrence River, and the fabulous theme parties.

The Musée du Québec is a Canadian art museum, featuring works dating from the 17th century to the present.

For those interested in antique furniture, there is La Maison Chevalier, which houses a collection of furniture dating back to the time of French rule.

CRUISING AREAS

The most popular cruising areas in Québec City are along St. Jean Street, north of Place d'Youville in the gay area. Plaines d'Abraham Parc, with its many wooded areas, has the most action during the evening.

Terrace Dufferin, a long promenade between the Citadel and the Chateau Frontenac, is also most busy in the evening, when the lights across the river from the town of Levis create an atmosphere of romance.

Another good spot for cruising is Lac Vert.

Always remember to be careful of police, and steer clear of public washrooms.

Québec City, Québec (418)

ACCOMMODATION/BED & BREAKFAST

727 Guesthouse
727 d'Aiguillon, G1R 1M8
PHONE: 648-6766, FAX: 648-1474
Nine rooms in a newly renovated, historic house, 10 minutes from Chateau Frontenac. Just around the corner from Québec's gay cafés, bars, and nightlife. Also offers a breakfast terrasse.
HOURS: Daily 24 hours
▼ ⚣

Bed & Breakfast in Old Québec City
35 des Remparts, G1R 3R6
PHONE: 655-7685
Old historical house (1831) known as one of nicest B&B's in Canada. Was originally owned by White Fathers (priests). Budget-to-luxurious rooms and spectacular views of the Saint Lawrence River. Ten-minute walk to gay bars. Brunch in an authentic Québecois atmosphere. Cosy greenhouse/living room for guests.
RATES: $75 to $130 with breakfast, in season
$62 to $130 with breakfast, off season
PAYMENT: cash, traveller's cheques, American Express, MasterCard, VISA
▼ ⚤

Le Coureur des Bois
15 Ste. Ursule, G1R 4C7
PHONE: 692-1117
The only gay B&B within the walls of Old Québec. Clean rooms in a historic stone house. Experience their famous breakfasts and Coureur des Bois hospitality.
RATES: $39 single
$58 double
$72 triple
$88 quadruple
$75 per day for one of two private apartments
PAYMENT: cash, traveller's cheques, American Express, Diner's, MasterCard, VISA
▼ ⚣ ⚢

Hotel la Maison Doyon
109 Ste. Anne, G1R 3X6
PHONE: 694-1720, FAX: 694-1164
In the heart of old Québec, Hotel la Maison Doyon is near the Québec people's life: near the beauties of old Québec and the nightlife of St. Jean and Grande-Allée Streets. Continental breakfast included.
▽ ⚥

BARS

Bar de la Couronne
310 de la Couronne, G1K 6E5
PHONE: 525-6593
[*Editor's note*: Some nights for gays and lesbians. Call first.]

Café Bar L'Amour-Sorcier
789 Cote Ste. Genevieve, G1R 3L6
PHONE: 523-3395
Cosy neighbourhood café/bar where both men and women are welcome. Daily specials from 5:00 p.m. to 7:00 p.m. — also serves European-style hot dogs.
HOURS: Monday to Friday 11:30 a.m. – 3:00 a.m.
Weekends 9:30 a.m. – 3:00 a.m.
PAYMENT: cash, traveller's cheques, automatic teller
▼ ⚣ ⚢

Le Drague
815 St. Augustin, G1R 3N4
PHONE: 649-7212, FAX: 649-0882
Le Drague is part of a complex including a café/patio and pub with cruising bar. A friendly French atmosphere.
♿ ▼ ⚣ ⚢

Male Bar
770 Ste. Genevieve, G1R 3L4
PHONE: 648-6766, FAX: 648-1474
[*Editor's note*: Same people who run 727 Guesthouse.]
▼ ⚣

Le Studio
157 Ste. Foy, G1R 1T1
PHONE: 529-9958, FAX: 661-0199
⚥

BATHS/SAUNAS

Sauna St. Jean
920 St. Jean, G1R 1R4
PHONE: 694-9724, FAX: 694-1251

Sauna Bloc 225
225 St. Jean, G1R 1N8
PHONE: 523-2562
▼ ⚣

Le Sauna Hippocampe Inc.
31 McMahon, G1R 3S5
PHONE: 692-1521, FAX: 694-0368
Located in the Vieux Québec (old city). Operating for 22 years. Seventy rooms, 50 lockers, 10 large suites — short or long stay. Steam bath, Turkish bath, tanning room, private bathrooms in some rooms. Warm welcome.
HOURS: Daily 24 hours
PAYMENT: cash, traveller's cheques, INTERAC, MasterCard, VISA
▼ ⚣

Café Zorba Restaurant

854 St. Jean, G1R 1R3

PHONE: 525-5509

Greek specialities, as well as pizza and chicken dishes.

♿ ▽ ⚥

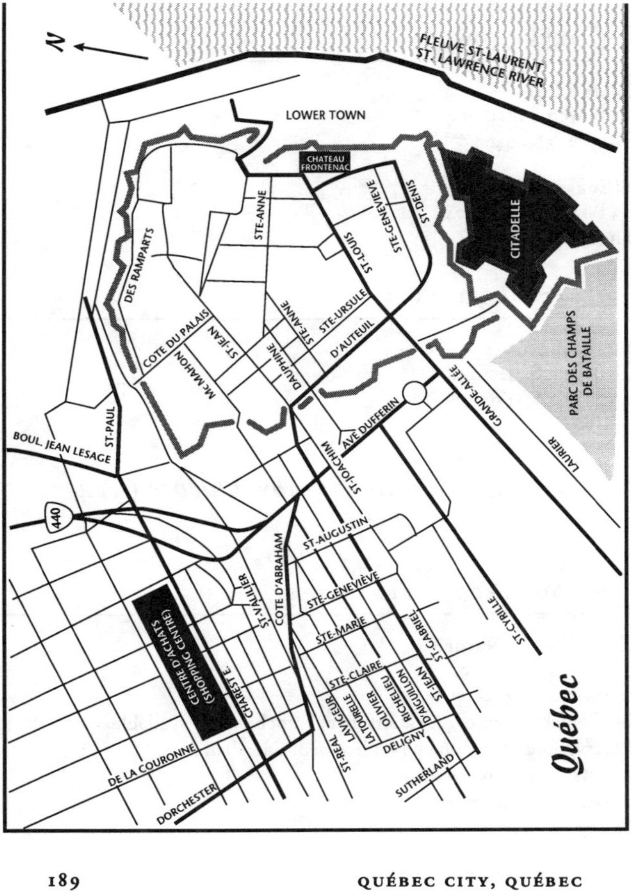

RETAIL

Importations Delta
875 St. Jean, G1R 1R2
PHONE: 647-6808

Sherbrooke, Québec (819)

BARS

Bistro Pub
17 Bowen S., J1G 2C4
PHONE: 569-6498

L'Evasion/L'Intrigue
13 Bowen S., J1G 2C4
PHONE: 569-1166

BATHS/SAUNAS

Sauna Lotus
15 Bowen S., J1G 2C4
PHONE: 569-1166

St. Alphonse de Granby, Québec (514)

ACCOMMODATION/BATHS/SAUNAS/
BOOKSHOP/LIBRARY/RESTAURANT

Bain Gai de Nature
125 Lussier, J0E 2A0
PHONE/FAX: 375-4765
Mail orders accepted. A catalogue in French only is available.
Reservations are required. Not licensed. Canadian food.
HOURS: 9:00 a.m. – 9:00 p.m.
PAYMENT: cash, traveller's cheques
▼ ⚣

St. François-du-lac, Québec (514)

ACCOMMODATION/BED & BREAKFAST

Domaine Gay-Luron
261 Grande-Terre, J0G 1M0
PHONE: 568-3634, FAX: 568-1130
Camping grounds for men only. Open the 1st of May until the 15th of September. Friendly atmosphere. Sixty sites. Fully licensed and light meals available. Phone for rates.
PAYMENT: cash, automatic teller, traveller's cheques
♿ ⚣

Ste. Marthe, Québec (514)

ACCOMMODATION/BED & BREAKFAST

Camping du Plein Bois
550 St. Henri, J0P 1W0
PHONE: 459-4646

Trois-Rivières, Québec (819)

BARS

La Maison Blanche #3
767 St. Maurice, G9A 3P5
PHONE: 379-4233

SERVICES

Gay-Ami(e)
C.P. 1152, G9A 5K8
PHONE/FAX: 373-0771

Entrevue, rencontre de groupe, brunch mensuels, comprehension.
HOURS: Daily 24 hours

Verdun, Québec (514)

BATHS/SAUNAS

Sauna Verdun
5785 Verdun, H4H 1L7
PHONE: 769-6034 for machine recording
HOURS: weekdays 11:00 a.m. – midnight
weekends 24 hours

Province of Saskatchewan

Among the vast fields of golden wheat in this prairie province are two major cities: Regina (the province's capital) and Saskatoon. Scattered throughout Saskatchewan are many national and provincial parks, forts, and battlefield sites dating back to the late 1800s and the Métis rebellions.

Indulge your butch side in northern Saskatchewan, where you'll find some of the best hunting and fishing in North America. The southern plains attract duck and goose hunters.

If leather is your scene, attend some of the rodeos or agricultural fairs held in the summer months.

The Provincial Sales Tax is 9 percent and the age for legal drinking is 19.

Moose Jaw, Saskatchewan (306)

SERVICES

AIDS Moose Jaw
Box 1795, S6H 7K8
PHONE: 691-0509 or 693-2003
[*Editor's note*: No office space as yet.]
⚧

Ravenscrag, Saskatchewan (306)

ACCOMMODATION/BED & BREAKFAST

Spring Valley Guest Ranch
Box 10, S0N 0T0
PHONE: 295-4124, FAX: 295-4121
A 1913 three-storey home with character, located in an isolated scenic valley. Tepees also available. Horseback riding and barn dances. Special annual gay-only weekend on long weekend in August. Reservations are

required. Food is unique home-cooked, country style.
RATES: House: $30 single, $50 double
Tepees: $17 single, $25 double
HOURS: Daily noon – 8:00 p.m.
PAYMENT: cash, traveller's cheques, MasterCard
▼ ⚧

REGINA: *A Brief Description*

The native people called Regina "Waskana," which means "pile of bones." When permanent settlers began arriving in the area, the Northwest Mounted Police provided not only security for the immigrants, but also thoroughly crushed the Métis and natives of the region. In 1882 the city became the capital of the Northwest Territories, as the area was then known. Christened Regina after one of Queen Victoria's daughters, it became the capital of Saskatchewan in 1905.

VISITING REGINA

For visitor information:

Tourism Regina
P.O. Box 3355
Regina, Saskatchewan S4P 3H1
PHONE: 306-789-5099

For gay visitor information:
PHONE: 569-0125

Regina usually experiences dry, pleasant summers, followed by cold and snowy winters.

GETTING AROUND REGINA

Regina is served by Regina airport, the city's one major air terminal.

Regina Transit, the city's bus system, costs $1.10 within the city. Call 569-7777 for more information on routes and fares.

There are double-decker bus tours available for both Wascana Centre and city tours. For more information, call 522-3661.

Regina also has Ferry Boat Tours, which provide a 30-minute cruise of Wascana Lake. Call 525-2148 for details.

GAY PLACES OF INTEREST

Gay Pride Day is celebrated in Regina, but the date of the festivities changes annually, and the celebrations are compartively small — sometimes gay and lesbian films are shown, a Gay Pride Fair is organized, along with a gay and lesbian dance. Call the Gayline at 569-0125 for more information on Gay Pride Day celebrations.

ENTERTAINMENT

In mid-June be sure to see the Western Canada Farm Progress show. The Buffalo Days in July/August celebrate Regina's frontier days. This event includes parades, rodeos, and square dances. Be sure to visit the domed Legislative Building, which has its own free art gallery (open daily), to see photographs, portraits, and other items relating to Saskatchewan history. Visit the Museum of National History, and the Norman Mackenzie Art Gallery, both in the same area. Also stop by the Science Centre.

CRUISING AREAS

The local cruising areas in Regina are located on Scarth Street and around the Cornwall Centre. Victoria and Wascana Parks are also popular.

Regina, Saskatchewan (306)

BARS

Scarth Street Station
1422 Scarth St.
Mailing address: Box 3414, S4P 3J8
PHONE: 522-7343
⚣ ⚢

CHURCHES/RELIGIOUS ORGANIZATIONS

Dignity
Box 3181, S4P 3G7
PHONE: 569-3666
An organization for gay and lesbian Catholics and their friends. Meets third Sunday of every month. Phone for location and time.
⚣ ⚢

Koinonia
3913 Hillsdale Ave., S4S 3Y6
PHONE: 569-3666
Inter-denominational, spiritual support group for gays, lesbians, their families, and friends.
HOURS: Second and fourth Sunday of each month at 7:00 p.m.
♿ ▼ ⚣ ⚢

SERVICES

AIDS Regina
2237 Smith St., S4P 2P5
PHONE: 924-8420, FAX: 525-0904
Offering AIDS prevention through education. Providing support services to people with HIV/AIDS. Condoms available and a library with books, videos, tapes, etc.
HOURS: Monday to Friday 8:00 a.m. – 5:00 p.m.
PAYMENT: cash, cheques, barter
▽ ⚥

Gayline
PHONE: 569-0125
HOURS: Tuesday and Wednesday 8:00 p.m. – 10:00 p.m.

SASKATOON: *A Brief Description*

Saskatoon is primarily a farm and mining region. The city was founded in 1882 by a group of Ontario Methodists, who planned to build a Methodist utopia on the 200,000 acres of land granted to them by the federal government. They named the region Minnetonka, after a local lake, but the name was eventually changed to Saskatoon, which means "Juneberry," in honour of the red berries that grow in the region.

VISITING SASKATOON

For information about the gay community:
PHONE: (306) 665-1224 (gayline)

Saskatoon's weather is extreme, with hot summers, and cold, very snowy winters.

GETTING AROUND SASKATOON

The city is served by Saskatoon Airport, located northeast of the city.

Bus service is provided by the Saskatoon Transportation Company, and the fare for a one-way trip is $1.10.

GAY PLACES OF INTEREST

Saskatoon's Gay Pride Week festivities are held in the last full week of June, including such activities as a presentation of art shows, gay and lesbian films, and an awards night.

ENTERTAINMENT

Events to participate in include a Winterfest in the winter months and a Folkfest in August. Folkfest happens on a long weekend with many multicultural pavilions.

Visit the Wamuskewim Heritage Site full of Indian heritage, artifacts, trails to walk and . . . buffalo burgers! Saskatoon boasts that anything that can be made from buffaloes will be, so why not give it a try? (Unless you are a vegetarian, of course.)

CRUISING AREAS

Saskatoon's cruising areas include the southern half of Spadina Crescent (including Kiwanis Park, also known as Bessborough Park), and Kinsmen Park.

There is no geographical area that serves as a gay community, though parts of Broadway Avenue are said to be gay positive.

Saskatoon, Saskatchewan (306)

BARS

Diva's Club

110 – 220 3rd Ave. S., S7K 1M1

PHONE: 665-0100

Entrance from a well-lit side alley. Nightly specials, great new location right in the heart of downtown.

♿ ▼ ⚣ ⚢ ⚤

BOOKSHOPS/LIBRARIES

One Sky Books & Resource Centre

259A 3rd Ave. S., S7K 1M3

PHONE: 652-1571, FAX: 652-8377

One Sky Books has a large selection of lesbian and gay fiction and non-fiction. The resource centre has files on lesbian and gay issues. Other focus areas include native, women's, and international development issues. Mail orders and special orders are accepted.

HOURS: Monday to Friday 10:00 a.m. – 5:00 p.m.
Saturday noon – 4:00 p.m.
September to May only

PAYMENT: cash, personal and traveller's cheques

♿ ▽ ⚤

CHURCHES/RELIGIOUS ORGANIZATIONS

AFFIRM
PHONE: 653-1475 (Bernadette)

Dignity Saskatoon
PHONE: 382-3669
⚣ ⚢

Integrity
PHONE: 244-5119 (Bill)

Lutherans Concerned
P.O. Box 8187, S7K 6C5
Write for information.
⚣ ⚢

PUBLICATIONS

Perceptions Newsmagazine
Box 8581, S7K 6K7
PHONE: 244-1930
[*Editor's note*: The gay/lesbian newspaper for the prairies.]
▼ ⚣ ⚢

RESTAURANTS/CAFÉS

Café Browse
269B 3rd Ave. S., S7K 1M3
PHONE: 664-BOOK
[*Editor's note*: Books, magazines, and a café.]

RETAIL

Out of the Closet
3rd floor, 241 – 2nd Ave. S., S7K 1M8
PHONE: 665-1224
Gay and lesbian merchandise including t-shirts, jewellery, magazines, and

greeting cards. A fund-raising venture of Gay & Lesbian Health Services.
HOURS: Monday to Wednesday noon – 5:00 p.m.
Thursday and Friday noon – 9:00 p.m.
Saturday noon – 5:30 p.m.
PAYMENT: cash, personal cheques, MasterCard
▼ ⚣ ⚢

SERVICES

AIDS Saskatoon

Box 4062, S7K 4E3
PHONE: 242-5005, FAX: 665-9976

Gay & Lesbian Health Services

3rd floor, 241 – 2nd Ave. S., S7K 1M3
Mailing address: Box 8581, S7K 6K7
PHONE: 665-1224
Providing support and services to gay men and lesbians on coming out, health issues, and more. Community resource centre. Also base of operation for the gay/lesbian line: 665-1224.
HOURS: Monday to Friday noon – 5:00 p.m.
Tuesday to Saturday 7:30 p.m. – 10:30 p.m.
▼ ⚣ ⚢

Gayline

PHONE: 665-1224
HOURS: Tuesday to Saturday 7:30 p.m. – 10:30 p.m.

TRAVEL/TOURS

Jubilee Travel

108 – 3120 8th St. E., S7H 0W2
PHONE: 373-9633, FAX: 374-5878
Retail travel agency with many years experience, member of IGTA. In-depth knowledge of popular gay/lesbian destinations, accommodations, and tours.
HOURS: Monday to Friday 9:00 a.m. – 5:30 p.m.
Saturday 10:00 a.m. – 5:00 p.m.
PAYMENT: cash, personal and traveller's cheques, American Express, MasterCard, VISA
♿ ▽ ⚥

OTHER

Gaymates
P.O. Box 3043, S7K 3S9
PHONE: 652-3399
Penpal/contact club for gay/bi men. Members across Canada.
PAYMENT: cheques
▼ ⚣

Yukon Territory

Whitehorse, Yukon (403)

SERVICES

Gay & Lesbian Alliance of the Yukon Territory
P.O. Box 5604, Y1A 5H4
Voicemail: 667-7857
▼ ⚣ ⚢

Tours to Canada

Odysseus Enterprises Ltd.
P.O. Box 1548
Port Washington, NY 11050, U.S.A.
PHONE: (516) 944-5330
FAX: (516) 944-7540
Toll-free: (800) 257-5344
Publishers of *Odysseus*, the international gay travel planner. Reservation service for gay/lesbian resorts worldwide. Specializing in European travel.
▼ ⚣ ⚢

Olivia Cruises and Resorts
4400 Market St.
Oakland, CA 94608, U.S.A.
PHONE: (510) 655-0364
FAX: (510) 655-4334
Women-only luxury cruises and resort vacations. Over eight thousand women have vacationed with us since 1990. Top-notch entertainment and staff on each trip.
HOURS: Monday to Friday 9:30 a.m. – 5:30 a.m.
PAYMENT: personal, traveller's, and cashier's cheques, money orders, MasterCard, VISA
Most trips are wheelchair accessible! Call for trips to Canada.

Out On the Slopes
P.O. Box 1370
Whistler, B.C.
PHONE: (604) 938-0772
Whistler Gay & Lesbian SkiWeek — Join gays and lesbians from around the world for a week of skiing and fun at North America's foremost resort. An annual event held the second week of February (4 – 11 February 1996).
PAYMENT: cash, personal and traveller's cheques, MasterCard, VISA

Wild Women Expeditions
P.O. Box 145, Station B
Sudbury, Ontario P3E 4N5
PHONE: (705) 866-1260 or (416) 535-0748

Offers women fun outdoor programs and canoeing adventures in northern Ontario. Enjoy the beauty and challenge of paddling through spectacular lakes and rivers. All equipment and food supplied, along with a friendly, experienced guide. Art programs and spirituality weekends are also held at our base camp. Over 200 acres with cabins, swimming and sauna.

Canoe trips from three to seven days in length (June through September). Locations include Temagami, Killarney, the Spanish River, and the north channel of Lake Huron.

Autumn and winter getaways as well: for Thanksgiving and Christmas, three days. Cabin accommodation. Sauna. Outdoor activities.

RATES: Vary. Become a member and save money.

For Canadian travel companies that are gay-positive or gay/lesbian owned, please see the travel/tour heading for each individual city.

Did we overlook you in this edition?
Do you know someone who should be included in next year's edition?
Please fill this out and return it to:

BENT GUIDE TO GAY/LESBIAN CANADA 1996/1997
Bent Books / ECW PRESS
2120 Queen Street East
Suite 200
Toronto, Ontario M4E 1E2

Listings are free. If you are interested in advertising, please contact us at (416) 694-3348 or fax us at (416) 698-9906. We intend to have an updated edition out every spring.

1. What is the full name of your establishment?

2. What is your complete address (street and mailing)?

3. What is your area code and phone number?

4. What is your area code and fax number?

5. Do you have a toll-free number?

6. Look at the headings in this guide for each city. Which of these headings best describes your establishment?

7. Describe the ownership of your establishment: Is it gay/lesbian owned and operated or gay/lesbian positive?

8. How would you describe your clientele? Gay male only? Mostly straight? Gay male and lesbian? Lesbian only? Mixed, including straight?

9. What types of payment does your establishment accept?

10. What are your hours of operation?

11. Do you require reservations?

12. Do you serve food? What type?

13. Is your establishment wheelchair accessible?

14. Can you give us any other relevant information? Please attach another sheet of paper if necessary.

If you have any comments or suggestions, please send them to the above address.

Across Canada, Whether you want a casual encounter
or something long-term: Here are the only numbers you need!
Cruiseline ✹ Xtra's Talking Classifieds
Try us for FREE: Toronto 925-FREE
Ottawa 237-FREE
Calgary 777-9481
limit one free membership per household: call now!